BEING

CW00816442

'Hard to remember how few women directors there were when I was cast in Di's first play. She was revolutionary, an actor directing, one of the company, conscious of a wide European repertoire and irreverent imaginative theatrical magic. Inspired by the subtle dance of words, she was just so excited to create a playful rehearsal room, her laugh infectious. Rehearsing in 1984, she had me standing outside McDonald's on a box haranguing hamburger eaters. I haven't stepped inside a McDonald's since. That's how good Di is.'

Mark Rylance

Di Trevis is a world-renowned director, whose work with Britain's National Theatre, Royal Shakespeare Company, and directing productions worldwide has deeply informed her knowledge of the director's craft.

In *Being a Director*, she draws on a wealth of first-hand experience to present an immersive, engaging and vital insight into the role of a director.

The book elegantly blends the personal and the pedagogical, illustrating how the parameters of Time, Space and Motion are essential when creating a successful production.

Throughout, the author explores and recycles her own formative life experiences in order to demonstrate that who you are is as integral to being a director as what you do.

Di Trevis has worked at the National Theatre, RSC, Almeida Theatre and The Royal Opera House. In 2001 she adapted, with Harold Pinter, Proust's *Remembrance of Things Past* which transferred to the Olivier stage in 2002 and won an Olivier Award the same year. She has taught extensively in the UK, USA, France, Germany, Austria and Cuba. Between 2003 and 2007 she was Head of Directing at the Drama Centre in London.

A Figure In The Distance, original illustration by William Schroder

BEING A DIRECTOR

A Life in Theatre

Di Trevis

Routledge
Taylor & Francis Group

LONDON AND NEW YORK

First published 2012
by Routledge
2 Park Square, Milton Park, Abingdon, Oxon OX14 4RN

Simultaneously published in the USA and Canada
by Routledge
711 Third Avenue, New York, NY 10017

Routledge is an imprint of the Taylor & Francis Group, an informa business

British Library Cataloguing in Publication Data
A catalogue record for this book is available from the British Library

Library of Congress Cataloging in Publication Data
Trevis, Di.
Being a director : a life in theatre / Di Trevis.
        p. cm.
  1. Trevis, Di. 2. Theatrical producers and directors –
  Great Britain – Biography. I. Title.
  PN2598.T73A3 2011
  792.092—dc22   2011006874

ISBN: 978-0-415-60922-7 (hbk)
ISBN: 978-0-415-60924-1 (pbk)
ISBN: 978-0-203-81636-3 (ebk)

Typeset in Times New Roman
by HWA Text and Data Management, London

FOR DECCA

CONTENTS

CONTENTS

PLATES

FOREWORD

Ronald Harwood

Di Trevis is an original. In her understanding of the process of directing plays she is, in my experience, unique in that she has transformed her craft into an art. She could not have done this consciously because as a director she is free of pretensions. Her process arises out of her personality which is without affectation and her intellect which is considerable.

Her concerns are for the most part with content not form, with the inner life both of the play and the performers. Like all artists she is intrigued by mysteries and directing is to say the least a mysterious business. *Being a Director* seeks to penetrate those mysteries but not always to solve them. Her method is to lay down clues, to follow trails, sometimes to make rules, all to entice the reader into the baffling world of theatrical presentation with its complex components of the playwright's intentions, fictional characters, the actors' personalities and individual interpretations. Add to these the function of design, light and movement and you have the elements which, to achieve unity in presentation, are finally in the mind, the heart and skill of the director. Here then is a sort of detective story because the director is, in this book, rather like a private investigator unravelling an intricate plot.

Directors only see the results of their colleagues' efforts because for each the process is in essence private. Of course the playwright, actors and technicians participate but they are seldom allowed into the secret, innermost world where the director's concepts and ideas are born and struggle to find life. *Being a Director* takes the reader into that secret world so it is not just a book for beginners wanting to learn; it will serve other professionals, celebrated or not, as an invaluable guide.

The book falls roughly into two parts: the technical, nitty-gritty of stagecraft on the one hand, and on the other, the illusive life of the work. For example, she is fascinated by time and space in so far as they influence staging. The choices of where or where not to place actors in relation to each other and to the audience is one of her many preoccupations and she reveals formulae that may serve as a basis for solving these difficult decisions. But far more importantly are her concerns for the choice and meaning of the play, the need to cast actors who will embody the characters and bring them to life and, finally, to understand that no theatrical presentation exists without an audience.

I have watched Di Trevis in rehearsal and, although she is cunning at concealing it, she is at heart a wondrous teacher. Gifted teachers are rare: they must, self-evidently, have knowledge they are eager to impart; they have to love their subject and, more importantly, their students to whom they should transmit their own enthusiasm. These gifts Di has in abundance. But she has something more to offer and that is imagination and instinct, those two indefinable qualities all talented artists share. In *Being a Director* she conveys the necessity of embracing both the real world and the world of the drama; above all the obligation to breathe life into the work.

ACKNOWLEDGEMENTS

My thanks go to Talia Rodgers who first suggested I write this book, to Nigel Gearing who was both a friend and advisor and to Niall Slater at Routledge for his editorial help and advice. Much of the book was written in Petaluma, California and I am grateful to my friends Kathy and Michael Lerner for their hospitality at their home on Cherry Hill and many happy sunlit memories. Thanks must go to numerous colleagues and friends for their help and encouragement: Daphne and Micky Astor; Merry Conway; Sam and Skye Dakin; Flo Hodes; Pamela Howard; Jane Gibson; Alexander Medem; Shona Morris; Christopher Peak; Graham Roos; Sylvia Rotter; Barbara Stone; my sister, Sarah Trevis; my daughter, Decca; my agent, John Wood; Tom Kuhn who supplied me with material about Brecht; Alice Knight who did photographic research; Helen Manfull, my assistant at State College, Pennsylvania where this book was completed; Dominic Muldowney who taught me about music and kindly married me; to the National Theatre of Great Britain for allowing me to use excerpts from *Remembrance of Things Proust*. I must also thank staff at the National Theatre Archive and the Royal Shakespeare Company for their help in locating photographs.

To the many actors, technicians, students and colleagues who have been at my side throughout my career, I owe immense gratitude and affection. Especial thanks must go to those who extended a helping hand to me in the early years of my career: Philip Prowse, David Macdonald, Giles Havergal of the Citizens Theatre, Kate Fleming (voice coach at the Old Vic), Litz Pisk, James Roose-Evans, Ian Charleson, Gary Oldman, Genista MacIntosh, John Willett, Peter Gill, and to Harold Pinter who at a later but no less vital moment helped me to go on going on.

INTRODUCTION

A long time ago I studied not directing, but anthropology.

The Nuer, a transhumant tribe of great beauty in the Nile Delta, now scattered to the mines of South Africa, were much studied by early British anthropologists who were puzzled when it appeared that the Nuer did not believe that sex resulted in babies.

When questioned further, members of the tribe grudgingly agreed that sex was associated in some way with the conception of a baby but that did not mean sex actually made babies.

'So what does make babies?' the anthropologist reportedly asked.

'Kwoth', came the reply.

'What', the anthropologist asked, 'is kwoth?'

The Nuer found it difficult to express exactly what kwoth was: kwoth meant ... the wind.

Did the Nuer believe conception somehow depended on the weather? No, they tried to explain, when they said wind, they meant something you could not see but which was there ... kwoth.

'Sometimes', someone added, 'it means the breath.'

'The breath?'

'Yes, the breath ... of life.'

Kwoth refers to both the intangible quality of air and the act of breathing in and out. It is like the wind, invisible and ubiquitous. But though kwoth is not these things, it is in them in the sense that you understand it through them. It is the breath of life in the sense that music is more than the wood and animal gut of a violin.

Years later, as newly appointed Head of Directing at a London University, I was summoned to a meeting to fully examine and justify the Course Document. This was a hefty file written by my predecessor in which were laid out all the details of how directing should be taught term by term, subject by subject, year by year.

I was among the first to arrive and was amazed to see a formal arrangement of chairs and desks in a horseshoe shape in one of the elegant reception rooms. As the meeting convened, I detected a horrible formality. When I walked around the room to shake everyone by the hand, I could feel I had infringed some unspoken rule of impersonality. And I realized everyone there, except me, thought this, the adjudication of a University Course, a very serious matter indeed. When about fifteen academics (most from quite different disciplines) had gathered, the very first paragraph – the Introduction to the Course – was criticized. 'It does not state', said someone, 'that at the end of this Course the students will be directors.'

I couldn't help laughing. 'That's because they won't be', I said.

'But they will have completed the Course', she replied. 'It is a Directing Course. It surely must state they will be directors.'

I knew then, so soon after my appointment, that my place was not in the fund-starved, bureaucratized, enumerated, box-ticking, report-filing institutes of higher learning. For directing, like so many other subjects studied at universities of the arts, does not require just three years of seminars and innumerable sets of marks. It does, granted, use a set of rough skills and I suppose this could be passed on in a fashion but – and how could I explain this to the horseshoe of poker-faced academics? – to really do it, to be properly serious and worthwhile at the job, requires more. I knew that they knew this in their hearts. At the same time they were trapped in a bureaucratic culture where the measure of everything, not its worth, is deemed important: a culture that values numbers above words.

The afternoon sun became hot. My head began to ache. I thought of the way I had become a director. Haphazardly, with things learned by the way. How did anyone become a kind of artist after all? The panel of academics talked on. They were under an obligation to follow government guidelines on education; everything must be subject to measurement, to outcome, to exit speed. Exit speed refers to the notion that you can judge the success of an academic course by how many students after graduation achieve employment in a certain period of time – a year, for example – in the profession for which they have been trained. Used as a measure of a good actor or director – or indeed most artists, in our culture and our economy – the concept is ridiculous.

Finally, after much discussion, it was agreed that the document should read: 'At the conclusion of the Course the graduates will be able to take their place in the directing profession.'

That is, they will know how to have sex.

But will they make babies?

So here, straight from the teacher's mouth, is how to direct:

- Decide to become a director.
- Choose a play.
- Read the play.
- Cast some actors who may be able to resemble what you imagine the characters to be.
- Rehearse the actors, getting them to move and speak to each other in various dramatic situations.
- Move them into a designed space and light them.
- Find some music to fill up the bits where scenes change.
- Show the play in front of other people who look at and listen to it.

There you are: that is directing.
And then there is ... the kwoth.

The best directing will always be about who you are, not what you do.

Part 1

DIRECTING:
THE PARAMETERS

1

SPACE

Space fascinates me. But no more than that magical moment when a human being enters it. Suddenly, the space is dynamic. Here, you feel, is the beginning of a story.

Think only of this: a figure moves forward into the empty space, stops, lifts his eyes, arches his neck up slowly, revealing the throat – that most vulnerable part of the acting body – and breathing out he falls to his knees. It is as if the spaces around him suddenly zoom in and out and the eye understands a multiplicity of meanings. He is on earth and above him the heavens. We are in a world where humans abnegate themselves to another world. The horizontal space suddenly expands, and above the figure there extends an infinity of ether. In an instant, a multiplicity of meanings. And in finding these meanings, we find what it is to be human. That is why we go to the theatre and why we make theatre: to express more fully what it means to us to be human – a figure in the infinity of space searching for meaning.

I can never forget the first moments of my first technical rehearsal of my first production – *Desperado Corner* at the Citizens Theatre, Glasgow – when all the details of the production came together for the first time – set, lighting, actors in costume moving through the space, music … and then, a torrent of speech. I simply did not know what I was looking at, where to place my anxious eyes and how to order the myriad sensations that suddenly assailed me.

The most fundamental question a director must ask as they contemplate the space, stretching empty into the distance or filled with the furniture of a nineteenth-century drawing room or the torn battle flags of Lancaster and York is, 'What am I looking at?'

Just as every gesture, turn of the head or direction of the foot in the human figure in the space becomes highly connotative, or filled with meaning, so it is with the object: every detail of its weight and mass, the gleam of its wood, the colour of its materials, proportion and line, the perfection of its symmetry, or the variety of its chaos, renders up a narrative once placed in the space. But what is even more interesting to any director must be what becomes of the space itself as it is dissected, for the divisions in the space behind and in front of the object or figure, to its sides and below or above it are at once filled with narrative possibilities and what's more they appear to change mysteriously before your eyes.

I often see a kind of panic in the eyes of young directors as they contemplate the actors in the rehearsal. They do not know where to look and what it all means. But seeing the potentialities of space can be honed by practice. Harrison Birtwistle, the composer, once walking with me in France discussing the opera *Gawain*, suddenly stopped and looked over to a flock of sheep grazing on an upland field: 'Look,' he said, 'no director could ever arrange the stage with figures as beautifully as those sheep are in that field, and look how it all changes as they move.' We stood and looked for a few moments and then walked on. Here was a man whose life had been dominated by sound, by what he heard, and in the order he heard it, giving me a simple lesson in how to look.

As soon as you have objects or figures in a space, you are dividing the space into different areas which have volume, height, depth, and width. In an instant they become symbolic areas for dramatic action, full of potentiality for the characters to express their needs within a scene. The objects and the spaces they delineate, represent what has to be overcome by each character to reach the other, not just physically but emotionally. In anthropology, we talk about distance in terms of actual space measured in feet, metres and miles and of *social* distance which is space as experienced. It is a short social distance to cross a room to a lover and it is immeasurably further to move through exactly the same space to an enemy.

So on the stage we should always look to the social distance the characters experience as well as the measurable proportions of the space. In rooms these spaces are delineated usually by pieces of furniture and the disposition of this furniture is really of vital importance to director and to actor: it is in crossing these spaces, appealing across the boundaries that the ever-changing interplay of dominating and dominated is expressed.

But the director should not think of these spaces in terms of the horizontal lines only. There is massive potential in the levels of height in the space. Every time a director sits down to watch the actors inhabit the space, they should dissect it as if it were a square tiled floor drawn in three dimensions – there are all sorts of heights to be manipulated too. The designer and director may have already built this into the setting in the form of stairs, rakes of the stage, steps or platforms, but the actors themselves can be encouraged to use the height in the space to represent their actions, standing figures dominating sitting figures, lying figures enticing kneeling figures, standing figures defying each other face to face – the alternatives are infinite. And such are the potentialities of space that the director must think too of what the perspective might express, especially on the proscenium stage where the figure at the forefront of the stage may gain power spatially over that at the back – or the figure at the back of the stage brought on powerfully through the centre of the space may command other figures downstage in the diagonals.

Geometry

I am not a mathematician and would have never imagined I would ever be interested in mathematics again once I had stumblingly passed my O-level in the subject. But as I became interested in space, geometrical shapes in space began to fascinate me in terms of a sort of spatial poetry, where some shapes were pleasing and others seemed to hold a meaning beyond their physical measurements. The anthropological notion of social distance as opposed to actual distance became more and more comprehensible as I watched the interaction of characters through space and I began to see what angles and shapes were pleasing or expressive.

Diagonal lines which intersect through the depth of the space and across the width are full of tension and dynamic, much more than the horizontal lines through a space. A diagonal makes the distance between characters greater even if the play is set in the confines of a room, and if you think in terms of the permutations the characters can make within a simple square or rectangular space through simply moving in diagonals, retreating and advancing, dominating and succumbing, moving upstage as another character takes the downstage diagonal, moving horizontally along the back of the space or at the front to take up a new diagonal, the potential of a really dynamic movement of actors becomes apparent.

With more than two characters in a scene the key shape to remember is the triangle, where characters can take the dominant position or stretch out or compress the triangular shape according to their character actions and their intensity.

A director should always be aware of the divisions of areas in the space. Divide it mentally into quarters or even eighths, for a grouping can expand from the upper right-hand square into half the space and then the full space, and compress again into another quarter of the space in the course of a complex scene.

There is enormous power too in the divisions of the space vertically and horizontally into something approaching *thirds* as, since the Ancient Greeks, those with visual and poetic sense have understood the potency of the power of three. This division at the point of roughly one third of the space gives us what is called aptly the *golden ratio*. This sequence occurs if you add two consecutive numbers from a sequence beginning 1, 1, 2, 3, 5, 8, 13, 21, 34, 55, ... The ratio, when you keep taking one of these numbers and dividing it by the previous one, keeps approaching 1:1.6 which is known as Phi. Throughout history artists and architects have found that the shape of the golden rectangle and the ratio of 1:1.6 within it and its various subdivisions, held a mathematical key to beauty. If you want to look at a golden rectangle, take out a credit card: it is a golden rectangle almost to the millimetre. It is there too in the Parthenon in Athens.

The subdivisions within this shape are deeply satisfying. At the beginning of my career I would find myself shifting figures and objects in a space until something clicked in my head. 'That is it,' I would think. 'That is somehow right.' I found only later I was dealing with the golden ratio of the space divided 1:1.6. Of course, you do not get out a ruler and measure positions to the inch. It is an approximation – a feel for pleasing divisions in the space, for a geometry of beauty. It is simply a feeling that instead of dividing the space in half, there is a more beautiful division to be arrived at. Look carefully at which points, for instance, as a single actor moves forward through the space, he is at his most powerful in relation to the audience. It will never be at the very front of the stage where he will appear weak and vitiated, like a bird perched on a wire. It will be just within the first third of the space where he will appear most powerful. Then see how it would be best to place a second figure on the stage behind him.

Even within the human body itself, this golden section is at work. Our appreciation of what is beautiful lies in the proportions of eyes to mouth to nose. You can see the golden rectangle merely by bending your index finger from its middle joint. The length from the lower joint to the middle will form the vertical of the rectangle and the distance from the middle joint to the upper joint will form the horizontal.

With more than two characters in a scene the key shape to remember is the triangle. When a character takes a dominant position you will find the triangle will be stretched out or compressed according to the various actions and intensities of pressure exerted by the other two.

Once you have groups of characters you can think of disposing them according to the status in the group. Who at that moment is the principal character? Are his henchmen grouped in the depth behind him? Do they face another group? Who is the principal there? Are the two groups disposed diagonally? Do the groups hold together or split apart according to the changing alliances and arguments within the scene? Do they then dispose themselves along different diagonals? Does one figure dominate in the end?

The actors will often quite naturally assume positions according to status and emotional emphasis or de-emphasis but the director should look with care to see if relationships cannot be expressed more dynamically in the space. Often what is vaguely felt by the actors needs to be accentuated and placed more dynamically across a greater area. Actors left to themselves have a tendency to cluster closely in a space and they often need reminding to spread into the space and take up more acute angles. There begins then a dialogue between the spatial relationship which emotionally releases the actors, and the emotional pressuring of the various characters which in turn alters their spatial relationship. You are aiming to discover with the actors a changing spatial pattern on stage which expresses in turn an emotional narrative.

With large groups of characters, especially in opera where sometimes you are working with a chorus, it is useful to remember the pleasing properties of the figures 3, 5, 8, 13, 21, ... if you want to dispose figures in ranks, rows or groups. You should also consider with large groups on stage, the beauty of stark geometrical shapes rather then amorphous groupings, vaguely based on naturalism.

But all this play with the potentiality of space must have an underlying meaning. You can never manipulate the figures in the space for the sake of aesthetics or variety alone. The director then falls into the trap of suggesting where the actors should move and the unfortunate actors are impelled to remember what they are to do instead of discovering what forces are impelling them to do it. After all you cannot really *dispose* your actors except perhaps in a complicated mis-en-scene with more than about five characters where some choreography of the traffic of the stage is eventually required. Actors working well together will dispose themselves, as it were *emotionally*. They will take their places in the space more believably if they have discovered their own sense of how their character feels in relation to another. You should allow actors to dispose themselves emotionally first and then start to finesse positions as the rehearsal develops. The full use of the space serves one purpose and one purpose alone: to express what the characters are trying to do to each other, how they comply with or fight the emotional pressures from the other characters, how they express their own pressures in turn – this

7

is the basic material of all drama and the steps by which the whole sweep of the narrative is constructed.

How the actors relate to the furniture also has innumerable possibilities. Blocked by a chair, winding frustrated in the confines of a small upstage area; turning while seated downstage to look longingly towards an upstage character, the spine curved and stretched; pacing like a caged animal behind a diagonally placed table; leaning languidly across the back of a sofa, arm stretched and cheek against the velvet upholstery; suddenly succumbing to rage and angrily pushing a chair aside to reach someone: all these many sensuous responses to objects and space give an actor enormous potential for gesture and movement.

The contre danse

One of the places you could look when thinking about configuration in space is the world of the country dance. These dances, which began in France as 'contre danse' – that is, with people in a line facing or 'contre' each other – are danced to the front in the direction of a throned figure – originally the King, but now referred to as the Presence. For our staging purposes, the audience becomes the presence. These are simple dances usually involving a walk or skip but in them couples and lines flow and intersect into the most satisfying and almost magical patterns. One of the simplest motions is when the couples peel off, one line to the right and one to the left, turning in a curve towards the back of the room. The eye follows the couples until they are just beyond the curve upstage and then is drawn back to a new couple as they process straight down the space. This turning to the left and right is sometimes called casting off. If, for instance, you have two actors in a scene, you do not have to have them head directly for an exit or exits. They can move forward to cast off on each side of the space, making way for further characters who are walking straight down the centre. Where they go depends upon the story-telling. They can stay somewhere in the space for the rest of the new scene and complete their exit at a later point. This cuts a long exit in two and keeps the action swiftly flowing. While casting off is taking place at the front of the stage, other characters can enter horizontally at the back and a completely new image of distant figures can be constructed.

Sometimes a new scene can announce itself by exiting actors casting off in a curve that sweeps right around and below characters who are walking down *each side* of the space. The new characters can begin dialogue across the width of the stage which could have had props and furniture already set in it, and then they come either into the furnished

space or in front of it. Of course, by furnished I do not mean furnished as in a realistic room but certainly containing chairs and perhaps a table or maybe even a couch or divan. If the audience's eyes are sufficiently diverted by the swift movement of figures across the diagonal or through the curves of the front of the space, complicated arrangements can be made behind them almost invisibly.

When I first went to plays at sixteen years old or so, I took it for granted that they should be set in rooms and that darkness or a curtain would descend when the scene was changed – by stage hands dressed in black trying to glide noiselessly on and off in a blackout or simply humping stuff around behind a curtain. Thus the rhythms of the theatre – the moments of darkness; the scene-change music, usually from a gramophone in the wings and a few loudspeakers; the settling of the stage as one set of characters exited and another set came on – seemed to proceed according to some unspoken law of theatre practice.

Then I began to see plays that were no longer set in rooms but in spaces – spaces with battleship grey walls hammered with silver studs where dynasties battled or princes begged for life; great circular disks with the abstract prow of a ship gouged through them where someone sang of the death of love. There even came to the Aldwych theatre a great stage-sized trampoline evoking the scorching hills of Andalusia over which black-clad peasant women clambered laboriously. This thrilled me because the theatre was presented as simply what it was: a space that evoked a setting but did not seek to slavishly replicate all its details. The movies could do that. We are in the theatre, it declared – now use your imagination.

Discovering the potentialities of space

The secret of understanding any theatre space is to move through it, measuring it with your feet and trying to gauge its atmosphere, because, whether we like it or not, bricks and mortar exude atmosphere and no amount of studying plans or drawing diagrams can substitute for how a space assails the senses. Everyone who has ever chosen a place to live, from a room in lodgings to a house in the country, is aware of this. You must get to know as thoroughly as possible what your spatial ingredients are. And it is not only the acting space and the way it can be related to the audience that should interest you, you should also study the route the audience will take into the building from the moment they enter the door. The director and designer should take responsibility for the whole experience of coming to the theatre from the moment the audience arrives from the street to the moment they leave.[1] Pay attention to the aesthetic of the foyer, how the audience are led into the auditorium – consider the images they first see, the sounds they hear, the quality of the lighting, the attitude of all who work front of house.

You must be sure too to look at the acting space from every vantage point in the audience and to keep this in mind as you direct scenes. It is always tempting to keep to the same position in the rehearsal room as you work on a production but you should move frequently while scenes are being run through to check what the experience might be like from all parts of the house. The present convention of stage management and director squarely in front of the actors is a leftover from the time when the stage was invariably a proscenium and you looked at it through a picture frame from the front. I like to think that in the age of the actor-manager there cannot have been so strict a demarcation between those who directed the stage and those who performed, since the leading actor and the director were often one and the same.

You only have to consider a conventional nineteenth-century theatre to realize how architecture reflects the class and cultural values of the society it was built for – the red plush, the hierarchical tiers and boxes, the separation of the audience from the world of the play by a frame, the orchestra pit, the bars and waiting spaces, the paltry number of women's lavatories (nice girls, they seem to suggest, do not pee). Then there are the utilitarian municipal post-war theatres, built one feels by committee with emphasis on cavernous scale, clean lines and often disproportionately vast stage areas invariably accompanied by a litany of rules and regulations. Some theatres suffer, in my opinion, from too much attention to the aesthetic of the auditorium. The Swan Theatre in Stratford-upon-Avon, for example, is very beautiful with its tiers of balconies and its rich wooden cladding but its aesthetic is so dominant that it tends to overwhelm any effect the stage designer might be trying to introduce. My eyes are so seduced by the honey-coloured wood and arched roof beams that I feel as if I am in an extremely expensive rustic kitchen rather than a theatre space. A theatre space should be like the libretto of an opera – judged not only for how it stands on its own, but how it can be transformed and only fully expressive with the addition of its major ingredient: music or drama. The black boxes and studios of recent years – intimate, ramshackle and transformative – have given way more recently to the use of non-theatre spaces often breathtaking in their scale, form and beauty but with concomitant problems of audience comfort, lack of lighting and technical infrastructure and sometimes a total disregard for acoustics, as if the modern predilection for the sound-bite and short film sequence had been translated into a theatre relying more on image than listening, more on sensation than language.

Acoustic

The director and designer can do much to control what the audience see and how they experience their entry into a space but there is almost nothing to be done about a poor acoustic. As soon as a director enters a non-theatre space, the acoustic should be the top priority not just the shape or scale of the space. Clap your hands and listen for the sound, the echo, the reverberation. What one needs for the good understanding of human speech is an almost dead or non-reverberating acoustic, for reverberation softens the edges of details, emphasizing the vowels and not the consonants so that for instance, an audience cannot tell exactly what word has been said; God or got? Even a short speech in a poor acoustic tires, frustrates and exasperates an audience, who are often unaware of where the problem actually lies. The *sine qua non* of the theatre is communication and no matter how tempting a space may look, never subject the actors or an audience to a struggle with a poor acoustic if you have any choice in the matter at all, for you will start with one and a half hands tied behind your back. Even in spaces designed specifically for performance, there are often acoustic problems. There is a notorious dead spot on the stage of the National's Olivier Theatre in London, while seemingly small spaces often need enormous vocal energy from the actor to reach up into the height of an auditorium or those seats that lie behind or above him, as any actor who has played the Cottesloe Theatre on London's South Bank will tell you.

Directors should see as many plays in as many spaces as they can. Get into the space as early as possible and walk around, looking at the relationship between audience and acting area, and how the height and scale of the space affects sensation.

Look at what happens to the audience's body language as they enter the space. Do they become reverential? Do their eyes lift? Do they breathe more freely? What happens to the sound of the audience: do they chatter or laugh? Are they light-hearted or solemn? Does the space inspire excitement or is it cold and alien? Be aware as you watch plays how effects have been achieved in the space and how the relationship of actor to actor, actor to audience could be changed.

Ask yourself if the potential of the stage space is being fully exploited; whether new entrances could be used; how the audience area could be invaded by the acting; whether the audience could be configured in a different seating arrangement. Could the actors move into the audience space and the audience be transferred to the stage? Could the stage be extended or other acting areas be used – the balconies, the sides of the proscenium arch, the wall around the orchestra pit?

11

Child's play

One day when working at my home in France, I heard my daughter in an animated conversation with someone in my study and wondering who it could be, I quietly pushed open the door and found her intently playing alone with her dolls' house figures in a new and exciting dolls' house she had discovered in my office: a model box of the Swan Theatre, Stratford. She carried on a monologue as she played, improvising a narrative and creating dialogue for her characters. They clashed and fought and fell on the floor and jumped up onto an upturned box of drawing pins and flew through the air to the upstairs balconies.

Although there is always a limit to purely theoretical musings about space, directors might find it useful to make very simple card maquettes of the different kinds of stages they are likely to deal with: the proscenium, the thrust, the apron, the traverse, the theatre in the round and experiment with the different configurations and relationships the actors could make in the space and try to imagine what the audience experience in these various spaces would be. Play with these as a child would. Do not make plans or organize blocking, simply enjoy the possibilities of the space with your figures freed from gravity and any physical limitations and get the space sensuously into your imagination.

Theatre in the round

Here you find a space in which the acting area is completely surrounded by audience. When you are working in the round you should not allow yourself to be locked into one spot in the rehearsal room during rehearsals. Move daily to a different part of the space to remind actors that in performance the audience will be in front, to the sides and behind them.

Also remind yourself of the fact that the backdrop to any image in such a space is the audience itself. It will be essential to use the cross diagonals and to note where the actors may come to rest without blocking the audience's view, usually where there are gangways. The actors should approach each other across the diagonals to meet in the centre, not face to face but left shoulder to right shoulder to allow blocks of audience to see at least one of the actors' faces clearly, and you should keep them moving so that the audience feel they have a view of all the participants in a scene and not just one.

The thrust stage

In a thrust stage, such as the Swan Theatre in Stratford-upon-Avon, the director will find she has a very narrow proscenium lying at the back of a stage which then thrusts out into the house, surrounded by tiers of seats. The actors, once they step a few feet from the back wall, have the audience behind, below, to the sides and above them. The back wall is a permanent fixture and its material, mass and colour have to be incorporated into the stage design or it has be covered with a design element but then any covering reduces the already narrow strip of framed stage. Then once an actor is on stage with the back wall behind them and in view of the whole house, they have to venture boldly into the thrust space, cutting through the depth of the stage to the centre or diagonally to the far corners where they can find a spot to rest which does not block the view for a section of the spectators, again usually gangways. The atmosphere of any play in this kind of space inevitably becomes restless since any moves along the edge of the stage have to be just that – always moving – so as to only momentarily restrict the audience view of the rest of the stage and the other characters. In such a space the centre of the thrust with actors diagonally shoulder to shoulder, circling each other to give each section of the audience a glimpse of their faces, and then advancing or retreating down the diagonals to the corners of the stage can become a repeating, if not inevitable, pattern. In order to find different levels vertically in such spaces, you often have to use the actors sitting or lying on the ground, calling lines from upstairs over the balconies, or have a raised level across or thrusting from the permanent back wall.

In Tourneur's *The Revenger's Tragedy* (Swan Theatre, Stratford, 1987), Michael Levine, the designer, created a vertical slope from the back wall through almost two thirds of the space, in the form of an enormous collapsed banqueting table. This gave the actors the possibility of working at different heights in the vertical by travelling up the collapsed table, but still left them with strong diagonals at floor level. I had, though, to give a lot of thought to the geometric possibilities of the space beforehand and spent many hours playing with figures in the model box – just as my daughter was to do – so that I had the spatial possibilities at my fingertips on the rehearsal room floor.

Thrust stages often have entrances downstage through the audience where actors are perforce visible. This makes a swift entrance or comic exit line difficult. It may be that lines have to be spoken or called on the move when the characters are not quite in or out of the space.

Mixed stages

Some stages are a mixture of two sorts of spaces at once. The great amphitheatre that is the Olivier Theatre in London, with raked audience seats ranged around the sides of the front of the stage, is at once a thrust stage at the front with a deep and thrilling proscenium space behind it. Once actors enter the downstage thrust area, you have to be aware of audience in front and to the side of them and of how intimate the front thrust part of the stage can be, as if you have been given a studio space to conduct the bulk of the spoken scenes and a great opera house behind it to make pictures and long entrances.

You can find a variety of possibilities in almost any space but it is important to thoroughly study it in three dimensions, not just in ground plan and make sure you have completely learned its geography. Then, of course, it is no good having a spatial vocabulary without it expressing the characters' needs and intentions, and the basic structure of the narrative. It is important that the actors become familiar with the potential of the space so that they can use it fully to express character and emotion. Actors often automatically begin working as if in a proscenium since it is traditionally what they are most used to. Most training scenes in drama schools are played out as if in proscenium, and most young directors learn their first stagecraft in this arrangement. Actors and directors take time to adapt their imaginations to the new demands of a less familiar stage. Take care you know some of the basic rules that your space dictates, and then and only then will you also be in the position to dare to break them and understand the consequences. This applies to much of the director's work in staging and with the text. Make sure you know the brilliance of the underlying conventions before you blithely dispense with them.

Above all practise and develop your powers of looking. Things of beauty and complexity are around you in every aspect of your daily life, from a flock of sheep in the Languedoc to scaffolding on a building site in Holborn or a windswept plastic bag caught on a piece of barbed wire on the lower East Side of New York: all these have stopped me in my tracks and set my imagination going.

2

TIME

Time, colourless and inapprehensible Time, materialized ... so that I
was almost able to see it and touch it.

Marcel Proust

In 1952, the American composer John Cage wrote a piece of music for
pianist – this is the first startling point, pianist and not piano – which was
called 4′ 33′′. It is very simple and at the same time complex. The pianist
enters, sits formally at the piano in concert mode and then proceeds to
not play the three movements of Cage's piece for exactly 4 minutes 33
seconds. He then closes the piano lid and it is over. What has happened?

Well, the audience has been forced to contemplate both what sounds
can be heard in a measured period of silence but also to experience what
that period of measured time feels like. How long an experience was it?
How does the tempus translate into chronos?

These two categories of time dominate a director's work. Tempus
from the Latin gives us the word temporal and denotes time as it is
measured. Chronos from the Greek gives us the word chronological
and denotes time as it is experienced. Your work as a director involves
the organization of tempus so that you have the means to more easily
perceive and manipulate chronos.

Chronos

In the area of chronos we enter a realm which is highly complex and
is subject to all the indefinables of an artist's skill, for here we revert
to expressions like the director's instinct, taste, feeling and hunch.
We might even extend it to that dreaded word talent: the indefinable
something that separates the individual from the crowd.

You feel what is expressive in a scene in your bones, in your gut or in your blood – the sense of what is true and necessary cries out to you from an imaginative and emotional realm: it is as if written in your memory and in your dreams. The young director often asks: where does it come from? how can I get it? The reply is always: you get it from yourself, from what you have lived and felt and imagined. Only you know whether you feel that life in all its pain and joy and variety is coming at you from what is engendered on the rehearsal room floor. You have to go with your feelings because you have no other feelings to go with: therein lies your uniqueness.

One of the things you really discover as you sit in the concert hall and listen to the Cage piece is the sound all around you within the silence. Cage wrote it after he experienced time in an anechoic chamber, a room designed to cut out all outside sound, and discovered that even there he could not hear silence. He heard two sounds; one was very high pitched and one low pitched: the sounds of his heartbeat and his nervous system. These two sounds are with us all the time and yet we rarely notice them, but it is in these deep underlying variations in the pulse, the heartbeat and the nervous system that we experience emotion and it is in our emotional reactions that time as it were materializes for us.

What the director must become acutely aware of is not the measured time a scene takes but whether the scene proceeds emotionally in truthful and convincing variations of pace and how it takes its place in the momentum of the play. These will never be measureable in seconds and, unlike music, you do not have a score with notes of dynamic – forte, pianissimo – or indications of tempo as in crochet equals sixty. What you do have – and this is as exciting as it is frightening – is your own authentic and instinctive reaction: is it truthful? is it free-flowing? does it allow us to enter the experience and forget time?

A good musical performance does not proceed mechanically according to an exact tempo any more than a play can. A useful musical term for any director to grasp is that of rubato which is an Italian term meaning to rob. Tempo rubato – stolen time – refers to the slight speeding up or slowing down of the tempo of a piece in order to be expressive and breathe life into mechanical execution. It can best be spotted in great singing for there is an infinite variation that comes from speeding up and then slowing down again, sometimes with the accompaniment proceeding at a more even pace. A scene quickens so that it might slow again, or slows all the more to emphasize an increase in tempo. There is a parallel variation in the tempo of human speech which minutely calibrates volume and tempo instinctively to relay meaning and emotion.

In fact the myriad variations of pace in any given scene – the to and fro of dialogue, the pause for thought, the sudden glance, the rising pace of argument – in all this lies the notion of rubato. What you experience in a play is a long sequence of rubatos, where movements are slowed down and sequences speeded up to give the event its believable and at the same time dramatic quality. Time flies for the audience in a correctly paced play and this will have very little to do with actual minutes and hours. The measurement of a play by stopwatch is a simple one, but by no means the only one. Remember Zall's second law: how long a minute is depends on which side of the bathroom door you're on.

A good writer is always able to grab the audience by the collar and haul them into time and place, but in the opening of a play the director has not only the text but also much else to juggle – the audience is wrestling with an avalanche of signifiers both visually and aurally and great care must be taken not to let the action gush shapelessly onto the stage. The audience subconsciously understands whether the director has a firm grip not only on the story being told but the story-telling conventions being used and can only surrender to the experience once they trust the hand guiding their eyes and ears into the world of the play. The good director has to develop the touch of a good lover – a reassurance that you are going to be more than all right with them.

Concentrate intently on leading the audience through the myriad of details that you want them to see, listen to and understand. The first minutes of a Shakespeare play, for instance, have to be looked at and listened to with great care by the director with, as it were, a newcomer's reaction, as the average audience takes time to be attuned to not only the period language but also its metrical formality. The director might have been living with it for months and imagine that is easy to grasp because the text has been analysed, spoken and heard so often.

The director's mantra should be: is what is happening clear? You cannot take the audience on a long and complicated journey until you have taken them firmly by the hand. I am always reminded of the children's radio programme where the story-teller asked 'Are you sitting comfortably? Then I'll begin.' Not only must the audience be firmly led into the story, they must go on knowing clearly every detail of it until the tale is told. Clarity does not dictate either a slow or a fast tempo, but simply the right and truthful one for every part of the narrative.

Tempus

The organization of the hours, minutes, weeks, months of preparation for a production is an essential part of the director's skill because it is only by a judicious organization of your time inside and outside the rehearsal room that you can hack out the space and calm to allow your instinctive judgement of 'chronos' to get to work. On one level this part of the organization of your time is easier. I often compare the preparation of a play to cooking a meal. The parallels are all there: you have the text or recipe, you assemble the ingredients – actors, rehearsal props, scenic mark-up, your artistic team, and then – and here is the gist of your problem – you cook the meal. Here theory goes out of the window and you are faced with human beings struggling to conjure something altogether greater than the sum of its parts. To continue the image further, you must juggle the heat, rearrange the shelves of the oven, taste for seasoning and get the whole thing into an appetizing and presentable shape for the hour the guests arrive.

But at least with a rough timetable you will give yourself some idea of what you and the actors might have covered by what date. The problem you will always be faced with, to return to my cooking analogy, is that with a recipe you are given oven temperature and cooking times, with actors you are not. They are engaged on a gradual process of discovery and discovery does not come in nice incremental steps but in strange breakthroughs, half-achieved notions and sudden creative shifts. The director must be utterly concentrated and painstaking, suggesting a change here or a de-emphasis there, listening intently for textual nuance, aware of the currents of feeling in the room, the beginning of the right impulse or a split second sight of a passing image that can be nurtured and extended. Relentlessly keep in touch with process rather than result.

Once you have a timetable and feel in control of the day-to-day calls, once you have glanced at the printed timetable the stage manager hands to you each morning with the calls for the day, you have to then play a trick on yourself and the actors. You should approach each segment of the day as if you have all the time in the world at your disposal. On the one hand, do not allow time to be wasted by lateness, over-theoretical discussion or last-minute coffees and outdoor cigarettes but on the other hand never bring tension about time into the rehearsal process. Keep the room disciplined by your own punctuality. Sit yourself before the actors with complete concentration and quietness: only have eyes for them. The work is painstaking, perfectionist and detailed with the rare bolt of brilliance and the relief of occasional laughter. No actor can be creative if there is tension in the air or a striving for quick results.

Have some modesty and respect for those with specialist skills: voice, movement, fight and musical directors. These members of your team come to you with years of experience in their special areas and a good director should give them sufficient time to practise their skills. Their work with the actors is under exactly the same pressures as yours. No two actors will learn to dance or throw a punch in the same way: more importantly neither will two characters. A good specialist will feed into the director's work seamlessly but for this to happen they must be introduced to the company early on as an intrinsic part of the process and you should allow time for this. Talk to your colleagues about their work well before rehearsal begins and try to juggle their time and yours judiciously. No-one – not an actor nor a specialist nor a technician – will ever say no to being given more time, but they must be given enough to work in a proper way and this involves respect for their expertise. I always claim to spend time to gain time. Establishing a sensuous understanding of the world of the play, getting the actors rooted physically and vocally will allow them to work better, more quickly and more profoundly in the space when they are finally in rehearsal with the director alone. It is no good calling a movement director in at the last moment to do a few dance steps: it shows a horrible incomprehension of what a dance, culturally, is. Explored from the beginning by slow accumulation it will colour all aspects of the production like wine through water.

In a mundane and business-like way, once the date of the opening night is decided a director can make a foray into time management. A look at any cookery magazine can give you a clue, especially those that abound at Christmas – where you are encouraged to think what can be prepared in advance – a week in advance, a day in advance and in the last minutes.

So a director should take a very cold and calculating look at a diary. Count backwards from the final day in the rehearsal room. You need to make a very frightening calculation: how many hours of rehearsal do you actually have? Allow time for proper breaks – your own are important as well as the actors'. Consider when you might have other meetings – technical discussions with designer, prop maker or stage manager; meetings about publicity, or the journey on stage of a bed or a chair or a vase of flowers; lighting discussions, sound and music choices – all these have to be given full concentration. Never, though, let them encroach on the most central and important consideration: your time with the actors.

So as you look coldly at the time at your disposal in the rehearsal room, start to consider when you should be arriving at a final run-through and pencil it in. Then you can begin to work backwards. Looking backwards from the final run-through you should be able to work out what days might possibly be given over to running the separate halves or several sections of the play. Then you will begin to see how much time you have to look in detail at scenes, the movement, the accents, the fights, the voice work and all that has to be prepared in order to tell the story.

Before you even go into the rehearsal room, try to calculate roughly the rehearsal hours you might give per scene or section. Never do this too rigidly as it will inevitably have to be kept extremely fluid. Scenes that you anticipate will take hours of work often come together quite easily while others that you think straightforward turn out to be very time consuming. Then as you get to the end of a play it often opens up new meanings to you and what you felt worked well in an early scene suddenly seems inadequate. Emphases, rhythms, dynamics, characterization, meaning – the whole things shifts all through the rehearsal period. But at least with this rough timetable you will give yourself some idea of what you and the actors might have covered by what date.

So what has to be built from the first day in a creative enterprise is the trust that you will all cooperatively achieve some kind of end result which will be more than the sum of its individual parts. Everyone has to trust a process which will take up its own space and rhythm and will be subtly different every time.

3

MOTION

Litz Pisk, taking me in my first movement class as a young actor with Stage Two Hampstead Theatre Club in 1969, walked towards me saying 'What have you got under your T-shirt? Oh I see now: it is your shoulders.' She understood in five seconds what was preventing me from the full release of my voice and emotions. There is an apocryphal story of Litz singling out a young actor as a group of new students at the Central School walked barefoot around a room. 'There is something going on in your body,' she said to one of the young men, 'let me see you walk on your own.' The rest of the class withdrew to the side of the room. The boy walked. 'No, no, I can't see', she said. 'Take off your sweater.' He took off his sweater and walked again. 'Take off your leotard', she said, staring intently at him. He removed his leotard. 'No. No. I am sorry. I must see what it is. Take off your tights', she cried. Reduced to a jockstrap, he walked yet again. 'Oh, I have it,' she said pointing to one of his bare feet, 'It's your right big toe.'

Many directors, often sprung from a literary or academic background, do not really understand what is meant by movement for actors: they confuse it with dance or some kind of fitness training for the actor. I am here not talking just of a ritualized, regulated, repeated movement in some form of recognizable pattern. I am speaking of actors' movement: where you do not seek to impose shape from the outside as in a dance step or the correct attitude. If the body is the instrument through which the physical life of a character or culture is expressed then that body must be articulate and capable of transformation. It is for this and this alone that the director should be aware of what can be accomplished by our great movement tradition specifically developed to aid the process of acting.

Actors' movement has flowed into our theatre culture from several parallel and overlapping sources in Europe – the mask and mime traditions of the Italian and French theatre and the developments from Russia to the Netherlands of work stemming from ballet and its many offshoots in modern dance and eurhythmics.

Jacques Copeau (1879–1949), a French director, actor and dramatist who founded the Theatre du Vieux Colombier in Paris, wanting to free the French theatre from its clichéd characterizations and exaggerated realism, realized that his actors should be trained not only to deliver the text clearly but also, through a skill in improvisation, to move articulately. Copeau's nephew, Michel St Denis, first joined his company as an actor and then having started to direct with his own company, the Compagnie de Quinze, arrived in London in 1933 and together with George Devine and Marius Goring founded in 1935 the London Theatre Studio. St Denis greatly influenced actors' movement training in Great Britain – his teaching being passed down through George Devine to among others, directors at the Royal Court Theatre, Peter Gill and William Gaskill who extended their influence to my generation through their work at the Royal Court, the Riverside Studios and later at the National Theatre. It was an amazing thought when I was taught to use mask by William Gaskill at rehearsals of Oresteia at the National Theatre that the rituals and rules of mask were coming down to me in a direct line from generations of great European actors.

Meanwhile, through the influence of Rudolph Laban and his work on the connection between effort, space and psychological states, and the dance theatre of Kurt Jooss who fled the Gestapo with his company first to Holland and thence to Dartington Hall in Devon, teachers of immense influence arrived in England. Yat Malmgren who later went on to found the Drama Centre in London with John Blatchley and Christopher Fettes, was invited to Dartington by Jooss and there discovered the work of Laban – a precise, detailed analysis of movement and gesture and the role it plays in supporting and extending the act of speech.

Born in Vienna, Litz Pisk was sent to train in movement as a child with the sister of Isadora Duncan and subsequently studied both design and dance. She designed the costumes and sets for the Viennese premiere of Rise and Fall of the City of Mahagonny which brought her into contact with Brecht and Weill. As Nazism took hold of Europe, she joined the list of artists fleeing to England, where first she was invited to work with George Devine and Michel St Denis who had meanwhile founded a school at the Old Vic. Eventually she became a most influential teacher at the Central School in London where my contemporaries Jane Gibson and Susan Lefton were both pupils. Both later studied in Paris with Jacques Lecoq whose work in clown and mask should not obscure his great contribution to pure acting. Together with Belinda Quiry who taught historical dance and Trish Arnold[1] who more perhaps than any other teacher before her understood the pivotal role of the breath and the connection between movement and voice, they have kept alive and developed this work conceived specifically for actors.

What cannot be rivalled is the very basic ingredient of the theatre: into the empty space walks the human figure. All right: How will he walk? What shape will his body make in the space? What shape will it make through the spine, the head, the arms, the feet? Actors' movement is not about stripping actors of the physical characteristics they have developed from childhood – like a mother nagging about a child picking up its feet or standing up straight. This training has nothing to do with striving for a pre-conceived ideal physique but with encouraging the actors' physical awareness: of how their bodies inhabit space and how they can arrive at physical readiness. Only then can they make imaginative physical choices. The choice is the thing. It is what Shona Morris refers to as the ability to 'shiftshape'. What has to be encouraged is not dance or fitness (although these can certainly aid an actor), but availability. What the actor needs to present in rehearsal and what the director works with is choice. Actors should be able to be sufficiently freed from their particular walk or gesture of the head so that any imaginative impulse can have an untrammelled route to expression. They need to be able to drop a lifetime of habit or retain aspects of it when and only when it is useful for a particular characterization. For this, they need to know what those habits are, where in the body they reside and how to neutralize or lose them if necessary: to make the physical life of the actor in Litz Pisk's words 'more alive, more transferable, more expressive'.

Physically, this means that actors work with the body – full of its own idiosyncrasies and personal characteristics – to arrive at a place of physical neutrality where the readiness is all, where nothing extraneous is happening. So that the spine is released, the shoulders dropped, the neck free, the jaw unclenched, the knees unlocked, the feet rooted into the ground, the breath flowing unimpeded. Actors are then fully open to whatever creative impulse springs from their emotions and imagination through their bodies to their very fingertips. But this involves a complex dialogue between an inner and an outer world for the more expressive the body, the more intense and infinitely complex the imagination and emotions become. An actor can move physically to an imaginative and emotional place outside the limits of the conscious mind. The body can make decisions that the actor has not rationally thought of. There is in the freed spine a super-highway to the imagination.

It was early in my study of anthropology that I discovered with a shock the theory that if you do not have a word for an emotion you cannot fully experience it. I discovered that the Hopi Indians had innumerable words for grass, for example, as a result of their intense relationship to the earth and their habitat. One of the major shifts in my thinking came when I was asked as a student to discuss whether 'family' was universal. The notion that even family (one of the most basic of kin groupings in Western culture which I had up until that moment taken entirely for granted) can take on vastly different forms in other cultures, came as a complete revelation to me. Then there were the carefully nuanced concepts of love in the Latin words 'amor' and 'caritas' and that marvellous little Japanese word 'mu' which denotes not no and not yes. With this realization came the liberating reminder that the structures and mores of our society are not universal or fixed or even necessarily desirable. And just as language can prescribe our experience so, I came to discover, can the physical expressiveness of the body: the symbolic words we hold in our muscles, joints and breath. When actors first experience a freeing of the breath and the spine, they must surely ask, as I did when I worked with Litz Pisk, 'Have I truly felt before?'

Getting the actors moving freely through the space can achieve much more than physical expressiveness, and much of the tremendous change and development this movement has brought to many aspects of acting lies in the most basic of pure movement exercises: the swing. The swing can be understood on a very basic level. When you swing your arm over your shoulder and allow the weight of it to fall, not trying in any way to impede its natural drop through gravity, it will take some time if left alone, to come back to stillness. It tends to swing a little like the pendulum of a clock until it slowly stops. And as the arm reaches its highest point, there is a split second of hovering before it responds to the force of gravity and continues on its downward journey. The swing is not about achieving something but allowing it – allowing an arm to swing back in its own time to natural rest. It therefore cannot be dictated – it has to be discovered by every individual. This simple rhythm of the unimpeded body gives an understanding sensuously to many aspects of acting since it involves an understanding of what is happening to the breath and physical impulse, that the inward and the outward breath has a downflow and an upflow and most crucially a delicious moment of suspension between the one and the other. It is in allowing this moment of suspension that actors begin to allow the text its rightful and natural rhythm; allow information and language to land upon the mind and body with full emotional impact before reacting; allow the voice to ring out in response to an impulse; allowing unforced moments of recovery after the expression of great emotion; allowing verse to flow forward without forcing it, allowing the musicality of the verse, allowing the audience's eyes to settle upon a moment of stillness on stage; allowing a moment where nothing happens except breath or suspension of breath.

An actor can learn to swing the arms, the legs, the hips, the torso. The swing can project you into sliding, jumping, leaping, falling. The work through the spine can take you down onto the floor or out beyond the horizon: it can access emotions and release energy. And it is in this word 'release' that the essence of the work lies. This approach to actors' movement does not imbue acting with struggle and effort, with externalized gesture. It releases the actor to natural ease, and the power to transform.

This is why it is essential that directors should consider carefully their own physical and vocal freedom and readiness. It is extremely useful to take some actor-movement training, not only for the usual reason given – that it gives you an understanding of what the actor goes through in rehearsal, how the simple gesture is often difficult to achieve – but much more importantly because it gives directors an insight into the landscape of their own emotions and imagination. In the end directing at its best will be about what you feel, how aware you are of the deepest of those feelings and the capacity and willingness to let that flow from your imagination to that of your actors. The atmosphere of emotional intelligence you create will be as important as the craft you exercise.

When I joined the Citizens' Company in Glasgow as an actress, I had no method of work to fall back on. I did almost everything by instinct. Luckily my instinct told me I had to somehow discover the physical life of the character, and when playing Joan Dark in Brecht's *Saint Joan of the Stockyards* I knew I had to find a way of embodying the young Salvationist whose concern for the redemption of the poor is later transmuted into political action. Throughout the rehearsals and all through performances, when off-stage, I wore an old-fashioned wraparound apron and carried a bucket of water, scrubbing brush and rag. When I was not on-stage playing a scene, I would get down on my hands and knees and scrub the backstage floor, then as my cue approached, wipe my hands, pull on my costume jacket and straightaway, full of breath from the effort of the work, step onto the stage for the next scene. This seemed to me the best way to 'feel' the character. When I started to work as a director, I tried always to create an atmosphere where work like this – below the level of words – had its proper place in the rehearsal room.

Part of the director's preparation before rehearsal starts should be to research the music of the time the play will be set. Once you have begun to fill the actors' ears and your own with the music of the time, you can also begin to explore through movement the physical life of the characters. How do these people walk? How do they walk to the music of the time? How will they dance? Will a stage full of those dancers give us a glimpse of the society we hope to penetrate? It is simply of no importance whether a dance actually appears in the final production or not. What better way to investigate a world than through the dance – not for the exact execution of the steps but for all else a social dance brings with it: the manners, the mood, the gestures, the patterns, the relationships?

A good movement director does not teach a dance in terms of simply technical precision but takes the actor into the sensation of the patterns, the sensuous feel of the partner, the relationship of the feet to floor, head to the heavens and heart to melody. If a director does not have the budget for a movement director, they should go and learn the dance of the period themselves and more importantly, the sensation of the dance and what it says about the society who danced it and, if at all possible, get the actors not only to learn the steps and patterns but to explore and inhabit the world it represents.

Let us take the social dance of the late nineteenth century: the waltz. In order to waltz you have to stand, move through the space: a man invites a woman to dance, the woman accepts and rises from her chair, perhaps taking leave of her companion. There are reverences, greetings, acknowledgements, handshakes, the return of partners to a chair. Work at this level involves not just the copying of a set of movements or mannerisms but a real entry into the spirit of society.

For an interesting aspect of the waltz is that the man leads. It is he who decides the direction of the dance, communicating it to the woman by exerting the smallest of pressures through the palm of his hand firmly pressed against her back. Many modern actresses find it almost impossible to submit to this sensation. They simply cannot allow themselves to be led. Everything in their experience cries out to them to adopt a less submissive attitude. But when two people waltz well together, the woman yielding backwards supported by the frame of the arms, the man taking a forward step between the legs of his partner, the sensation is almost one of weightlessness and telepathy – as if their bodies speak to each other. You move as one.

Of course, that the lead is taken by the man does no doubt reflect the patriarchal tendency of a society. But it could also be argued it reflects a perfectly natural sexual instinct. In the twentieth century, the 1950s brought us rock 'n' roll, originally Afro-American slang for sex, with the dance directed by the touch of hand as the couple rocked back and forth and the woman twirled, jumped around the man's thighs and sometimes slid on the floor through her partner's legs. Then came the Twist, where couples still faced each other gyrating their pelvises but were not in physical contact. Take an anthropological look at the increasingly anarchic modern social dances of the turn of this century where there is no physical contact between the partners, and each gyrates in his own space. This surely must reflect burgeoning feelings about liberation, the refusal of women to be automatically led, and the need for individual expression. A simple look at the mosh pit at any gig or the seething chaos of a rave, can give you a startling picture of the divergent struggle now being waged between a desperate need for communal experience and at the same time anarchic isolated outbursts of frenzy: a society where the individual is in the worst throes of anomie.

In the learning of a dance there are always new physical sensations to discover. For instance, you cannot begin to move through the Elizabethan dance of the pavane without finding strength in the spine, intensity in the eyes and flexibility in the feet. This inevitably involves some concentration on pure movement training, where the actors work more abstractly in the space or on the floor, concentrating on freeing the spine, or swinging arms, legs and upper body, working through the feet and ankles to make them more supple. This will give a clue to more than the dance, for these particular physical strengths will be reflected in everyday social gesture, and notions of posture and beauty. When Elizabethan men began to dance the volta, where enormous physical strength is needed to lift the partner and to jump high in the air, the strong masculine leg became a measure of beauty, especially well-developed calves and broad shoulders tapering to a small waist which was accentuated by the cut and corsetry of the bodices.

The relevant dance can help the actor ingest into every aspect of his physical life a culture and a period removed from our own. The actors find a way to discard the teeming twenty-first-century life outside the theatre, free themselves from the body language of blue jeans and sneakers and enter another world.

The shoes and clothes an actor wears for rehearsal are therefore of immense importance. Actors cannot easily enter the world of the late nineteenth century or the Restoration period in a pair of squashy-soled trainers which lift them away from the sensation of the floor, and so cushions the action of walking through the foot from heel to sole that the spine sags and slumps. The actor needs to get a pair of thin leather-soled shoes and wear an appropriate jacket, shirt and tie if he is to begin a physical and imaginative transformation from our age to another. Similarly women need to get into the right length of skirt as quickly as possible, to wear in rehearsal the correct period corset and leather-soled shoes with heels. They need to handle gloves, peignoirs, parasols, hats, fans and long trains for weeks if they are to use them with ease in performance. Many young actors are encouraged in their drama training to build their own rehearsal wardrobes. At Drama Centre, London where Yat Malmgren set much of the agenda, the actors are trained to concoct their own costumes for their first year performances and these are judged as closely as the performance itself as they give a clue to how well the actor is in touch with the culture and the physical life of the character. Some actors come to the professional rehearsal room ready with appropriate clothes and props, but as good as this is in setting a tone of preparedness and play, the responsibility for rehearsal costume and the right prop or clothing accessories lies with the director. It is the director who can set up an atmosphere of work in which such preparation seems only right and proper and can alert stage management and wardrobe departments to the need for such provision.

When, very early in my career, I directed Auguste Strindberg's play, *Miss Julie*, the actor Peter Wight, playing Jean, simply could not start rehearsing one morning. 'Someone has moved my acting jacket', he wailed. He was lost and could not even remember his lines. Once we found it, he put on the jacket, walked in character into the space, and remembered the part perfectly.

Once you have the actors moving through the space in a dance, it is a small step to get them moving into other areas of activity – from the waltz to a walk in the woods, sitting at lunch outside, or lighting a candelabra. The dance infuses all the other gestures. In the pavane with which Jane Gibson and I began work on *The Revenger's Tragedy*, the actors progressed forward to the muffled beat of a drum, perfectly balanced on heels rising and falling and reverencing to the Duke. One of the actors in rehearsal hesitated, stopped and laughingly said, 'Oh Jane, I always get that bit of the dance wrong.' Jane, her face impassive, replied, 'In this world you don't make mistakes or if you do, you never let anyone see. It could cost you your life.' Jane had no doubt learnt from Litz Pisk her capacity for contagious seriousness. The atmosphere became charged: it wasn't about the dance any more but about the hideous nightmarish quality of the court. The actor now concentrated on dancing it faultlessly. It was a short step to an exercise in which actors tried to make secret assignations with each other while dancing; that an assassination was decided during the dance – the group unnervingly arriving, not by words but by eye contact and direction of head, at a chosen victim. In fact, the pavane became a stylistic thread through the whole production: the masque of characters Tourneur indicates at the beginning of the play was easily transformed into a parade of dancing couples side by side, eyes concentrated, control immaculate, treason teeming through their brains; and the masque at the end of the play was a pavane too, danced with skulls that flew through the air as the welter of murders was unleashed.

A sensitive movement director or a director sensitive to movement can therefore help in many areas which seem not specifically to do with movement or dance. They can often spot exactly what is limiting an actor vocally or emotionally – the tense jaw, the jutting neck, the locked knees, an arched spine, or indeed the errant big toe.

Part 2

DIRECTING: THE SPECIFICS

4

DECIDING TO BE
A DIRECTOR

Many years ago, I was working at the Royal Academy of Art helping young directors with their film projects, when Stuart Hood, their professor, came upon me one day, when I had some time to spare, sitting with a blank sheet of paper, trying to write down some thoughts on an idea that was just beginning to form in my mind.[1] He stood behind me as I held my pen over the paper and I sighed. 'I find starting things,' I said, 'so difficult.' He laid his hand on my shoulder. 'There come moments in life when what you have to exercise is not talent but willpower. You have to find nothing else at the moment but the will to start.' So I do not know where the muscle of will resides but you have to find it and exercise it.

Begin to be a director – and begin alone, if needs be. It is not magic; it is an acceptance that no-one can read your mind, no-one can know you even exist unless you find a way to tell them – and nearly always there will be a way and you have the sole responsibility to find it. 'A cooked chicken never flew through the window,' I always say. Nothing will magically come to you. Go out and find it.

Forget the usual trajectory that takes people from the bottom to the top of a profession over time, the gradual increments in salary and seniority over younger, less-experienced colleagues. Theatre just does not work like the legal, medical or other professions. You will be deciding less upon a career than upon a vocation. At base you are casting yourself as a maverick in society. Do not fear but embrace this notion. What you should come to terms with from the start is that in the harsh economics of the real world there is really no such thing as a career in the theatre: what you embark upon is a way of life – sifting your choices, pondering your decisions and directing your energies to what will serve to give you a set of heightened sensibilities and an outsider's way of looking at the world. There will rarely be regular employment or riches. At each bend of the very winding road that will be your professional life, you will come upon mysterious impasses and the quite incredible feeling that you are having to begin all over again. In fact, look at the word 'career' and take it in its literal meaning: your working life will be a jolting, hardly controlled, bumpy ride, often downhill. Not that this should dishearten you.

And take a look at that word 'dishearten' in its deeper sense and remember never to allow the heart to be taken out of you. Do not let the exigencies of the job take away the beat of life, the emotional openness within you. Protect those innermost feelings – the dreams, the intuition – for these are the inestimable treasure that will make you unique, the profound gift that any artist brings to the work – a sense of the personal.

In fact, it is useful to think of yourself as two connected but separate entities. You are your inner self, full of sensitivities, aesthetic yearnings and fervent imagination and you are a worker in that most pitiless of contexts, the market place. You are the sensitive self who directs, and you are the much tougher cookie, the director. You have to develop a set of skills for directing and another for being a director. Sometimes you have to serve the one and many times in public you have to present the other. It helps to separate them.

In the context of the market place – being a director – you can arm yourself with something of a carapace. You can face up to failure and shrug it off, you can present yourself with the efficiency of any other job applicant, you can make phone calls, try to arrange meetings, raise money, negotiate rehearsal-room rents. You can stay civil and un-bitter even though you feel personally rejected. You can – and must – do something completely practical and workman-like for your career every morning of your life. This will also exercise an organizational ability that is part of the tool-kit of any good director.

The other self – the inner one – you should look after, and you must honour. After all, you did not make your talent, you were given it by an accident of fate – and you should protect it. Be wary of envious friends, confide only in those who understand and nurture your development, and hone your willpower.

You will work without knowing whether your work will see the light of day, work sustained only by hope. For you will enter the world of speculation – of perseverance, of e-mails and faxes, and meetings and silences, ideas and doubts. None of our cultural institutions is escaping the cold hand of cost efficiency, line management, cash flow. 'Have you,' theatres will ask, 'an idea for us?' Behind that question lie planners and budgets and box-office predictions. Freelance directors do not use money for their speculations. They have half-perceived visions, feelings, hunches. They have favours to ask of friends. They have days of imagining scenes and sketching out cast numbers. They have lists of actors to suggest – actors who might be free, might be interested, might be box-office. They have weeks of reading plays they will not get to do. Of dates postponed, changed, cancelled. Of budgets cut and trimmed, of ideas dismissed, extolled, ignored, grabbed with hungry hands. Of meetings where the theatre office is a market place and you have to set out a stall and sell, when what you have to sell cannot be held in your hands. Any young director should prepare for this other world: the world of speculation.

What you have to face is how to provide yourself with a conduit for your ideas, and an attitude that will allow what is insubstantial to come into being the moment an opportunity arises. And you have to address the problem of how to make opportunities arise. You will career from one unconnected opportunity to another – and since life is lived forward and only understood backwards, only in retrospect will you see that it all had some kind of creative shape. I am often asked by young theatre practitioners how to begin and I am tempted to put it another way. How do you go on? It is the ability to keep on going that you must develop in spades-full.

The writer has the blank sheet of paper, the composer the unfilled staves, the painter a blank canvas – the young director needs actors, a rehearsal space, time, a theatre. You do not even have the direct relationship with process that so many other artists have – you cannot work alone – you cannot pick up a brush or tune a violin, you need others. You are often reduced to your domestic setting and your mind – if you are lucky a mind full of unrealizable fantasies and half-formed ideas. So what to do?

Society loves its artists when they become famous. They cannot wait to buy a painting that will increase in value. They like to say they know you when you have your name in the newspaper. But the unknown artist, the struggling artist, has no value for most of society – after all they are of no measureable economic worth. You will only have yourself and your energy and your powers of communication and behind all that you have an act of will.

Any trained actor spends a major part of his early training on emotional and sense memory, finding out who he is, digging down into his feelings and experiences. The same should apply to any director. In the end the measure of your talent will not lie in stagecraft or learnable skills, it will depend upon whether your work pulses with emotional insight, individual aesthetic, your simple human understanding.

So where can you begin? No-one is going to knock on your door and say that they have heard you want to be a director and they are there to help. Yat Malmgren used to say that the first act of creativity was to sweep the rehearsal room floor. You start, in other words with something simple, something practical and above all possible, and from that simple basic beginning a complex of developments will flow. Look within yourself.

Whenever I find myself sunk into the mundane materiality of life, and need to inhabit the more open spaces of my imagination I attempt to jumpstart my creative processes. I do the mental equivalent of sweeping the floor. You will find you invariably have in your head a perfectly good set of aims and ideas for work but they simply need to be realized. Thoughts somehow only become fully realized by putting them into words. I start by trying to give myself a set of questions, which I write down in a kind of formula which goes:

- What do I need to read that I am not reading?
- What plays do I want to do that I am not doing?
- What ideas do I have that I have not expressed on paper?
- What do I need that I do not at the moment have?
- Where do I wish to go that I am not going?
- Who do I wish to know whom at the moment I do not know?

You can make up your own formulae: after all, you can sweep the recesses of your mind and memory any way you choose as long as it prepares you for work.

It is really important not to censor yourself as you write down your thoughts and to allow yourself to go from the mundane to the fantastical.

You might realize at the beginning of your list you want a new light bulb for your desk lamp. You might at the end of it have reached deeper into your unconscious yearnings and realized you want to spend a summer in Provence. Do not underestimate your powers.

One winter I wrote a list including both these wishes. Half an hour later I went out and bought light bulbs and sat that night writing in a decent light for the first time for three months. The following summer when offered a production of Athol Fugard's Hello and Goodbye with rehearsals in August, remembering my transient fantasy, I borrowed a tumbledown house from a friend, persuaded the two actors, Jim Hooper and Annie Hayes to spend a week's rehearsal pay on a cheap fare to the South of France, and rehearsed the play for two weeks in a Provencal vineyard and a barn. None of us has ever forgotten this charmed experience.

For what you do is write what practical actions you can take to bring your agenda nearer, and then prioritize them and give yourself tasks for the next weeks or days. On at least one of them, take immediate action. Pick up the phone. Walk out the door. Make something happen.

You will soon realize that there is a project you have longed to do and there is a way of initiating it. And initiating is the key word: set something into being like a ticking clock and edge it forwards by small increments. It is the creative process you must learn to love and not the result. My best ideas have always had buried within them a simple practical first step: I can see a way to begin something and only vaguely how the rest might develop from there. But I make that first step and watch with amazement how the tortuous process towards realization evolves over the months and years.

And consider carefully how to set about achieving things.

So many young directors and actors are told to write letters, but the letters they write must be realistic. You cannot write to a leading theatre and ask if you can do a production of a three-hour epic and expect to get the job by return of post. I get letters all the time, frequently asking if I might take on someone – a complete stranger – as an assistant. It is highly unlikely I can give a satisfactory answer. I can put their letter in a file and tell them I have done so. And I can look at the file occasionally and suffer a pang of regret. They meanwhile might think they have done their best: they have written me a letter. But is it the best way?

If you want to work with a director you should get to meet them, if only for a minute. You should know their work. See their plays – in preview, if possible. They will invariably be in the theatre on those nights. They will be busy and tired, but they will be there. You could be bold and simply introduce yourself if you see them at the bar or ask an actor or technician to introduce you. Tell them how much you enjoy their work, as long as you sincerely do. Or leave a note at the stage door asking if they can spare you a moment. Do not stalk them: simply try communication as one artist to another. When you do write, ask for five minutes of their time, not the moon. Always ask yourself: what can this person in all reality give me?

Once they have put a face to a name, then is the time to write and ask whether they might be looking for an assistant or might allow you to observe them at work.

If you get a meeting with someone, think carefully what can realistically be expected from it: it will never be fully what you want but it could be a small step on the way to what you want. At the very least you might know that you have reached a dead end and save yourself a lot of futile effort. A young artist should take a long-term view. Meetings at the beginning of a career often only come to fruition years later.

In the short term, you might get to have a cup of tea with someone who recognizes something in you. In my experience I have found those at the very top of their profession the most accessible: the more talented, the more accessible. Talent has given them confidence and they have retained their heart. When I was a young actress, the most famous of the casting directors, Mary Selway, often picked up the phone personally. When I first phoned her office number, recovered from the shock of actually getting straight through to the famous woman herself, stammered out my name and that I had just arrived in London, she said simply: 'Come and have a cup of tea with us next Thursday.' She liked actors. She was always on the lookout for the next exciting one. Actors were her job and she knew it. Actors are your job.

You need to get to know as many actors as you can – both through their work and personally. They are also usually around after the show and I have never met an actor who dislikes being praised for their performance. Actors are often very amenable to talking about how they have worked on a part. And they are the best of company. I find there is nothing in the world as fascinating and sheer fun as a group of actors and they are the bravest and bonniest of human beings. I loathe it when directors talk disparagingly of actors: they are the bricks with which theatre is built. Respect them and love them and you will be re-paid by effort, passion and perseverance. If you make friends be honest about the relationship. One day they might want to ask you for a job. Make a little rule: they can ask and you can give it, or you may simply say no and proffer no explanation. If they can accept that, you can be friends without too many professional complications.

You should keep a log of all the productions you have seen, what you liked and how you think certain things were achieved. It helps when you meet an actor if you remember roles they have previously played, productions you first saw them in; no actor worth the name does not want to meet a young director who might be a future employer.

It is important that you practise saying to people, 'I am a director.' Say it often enough and you will even believe it yourself. Define yourself in order to get the world to define you. Each morning, look over your lists and ideas and do at least one purely practical thing to move your career forward: make a call, read a play, learn a dance, look at some paintings, listen to some music. Best of all, organize some actors in a project.

Most importantly, start to construct a directing language for yourself. A young director should do some acting. You must understand the difficulty of acting from the inside. All the time ask yourself what kind of suggestion would be of help, what is an actable note, why are seemingly simple things difficult to do and what kind of process you are going through.

If you have to get a job simply to earn money, set aside a percentage of it for career development: a grandiose term but an important resource. This money is for tickets, classes, journeys, books, days of dreaming and doodling, pencils, magazines, music. The thought of this percentage set aside for yourself and your future will help you out of bed for early morning shifts and give an element of creativity to laborious jobs.

Even if you cannot get the resources together for a production, at the very least you can run play readings or scene study in your own house or apartment. The internet is useful in this respect. Young colleagues of mine announce the play and the time and ask for actors. They ask each of them to print out the text of the play. Starting late in the afternoon with a rehearsal, they then give some simple notes, practise their listening skills and then have a reading in the evening. Throw in a cheap supper, get the actors to bring drink or a dessert and you have a social and professional event that will pay you back a hundred-fold.

The most important thing for a director to do is to direct. Direct even if it is two actors in an empty garage; soon it will be four in a village hall and before you know where you are it will be in a ramshackle theatre somewhere and you will be learning your trade. Read every new play you can get your hands on and when you find one that truly, deeply moves you, get to meet the author, beg or borrow the money to buy the rights and get going.

But behind all this should reside a feeling of entitlement: you should assume you belong to the ranks of the theatre no matter how lowly a start you are making. For most of us the transition from our origins to our life in the theatre began with only the desire and the dream. Nearly everyone's journey from their beginnings into the profession was the longest they ever made, and in places along the line they received a helping hand, a moment of recognition, an understanding word. They retain at heart, if not irretrievably embittered by the struggle, a real reservoir of fellow feeling for anyone setting out or going on going on. In time you too will, I hope, extend a helping hand to a young unknown. Karen Blixen, the writer, was once asked how she jumped a fence on horseback. She said that she threw her heart over first. The rest followed.

5

CHOOSING THE PLAY

Years ago the journalist Katharine Whitehorn, on reading in the problem page of a newspaper a letter from a young woman married to an older man and in love with her stepson, realized that her reply could consist of one word: Phaedra.

That young woman, if she had only known it, might have understood that her dilemma – secret, shameful and tormenting – was the stuff of myth. Agony such as hers had been played out in the amphitheatres of Greece, where everyone understood the gods themselves inflicted these feelings on womankind. A 3000-year-old play would have spoken directly to her, telling her her own story and placing her sad domestic tale in the context of age-old human tragedy.

In every play that you direct, there must be something that speaks to you, to your story, to your biography. To direct Phaedra, you do not have to have loved your stepson, you do not even have to have a stepson, but you do have to know what it might be to love what is forbidden, out of reach or untouchable. Instead of Phaedra, someone who knew what it is to love in vain could have found her story in *A Month in the Country* or that heart-breaking scene where Varya waits for a proposal that never comes in *The Cherry Orchard*.

There must be a moment in the play that comes alive to you, leaps off the page in an image or a sound: a moment where you understand its very essence. If you cannot find such a moment in a play, be wary of touching it. You will never quite succeed. Your production might be efficient, it might be workman-like but it will never have that indefinable pulse of truthfulness that moves an audience of strangers. And at the beginning of your career, that is what will set you apart – even if your work is unaccomplished technically, even if your actors are not of the very best, even if the theatre is obscure and hard to find, it will be this which will set you apart from the crowd. You will find that same indefinable spark in young actors, painters, writers and musicians: the sign of the artist.

It is especially important to choose a play that you are passionately interested in at the beginning of your career when you will be trying hard to convince people to let you do it. Your passion is what will convince them, not your track record. Your feeling for the play will give you the edge over other mere workhorses, for you will bring what is personal, truthful and unique to your vision of it. Your actors will respond to it, your designer will be inspired by it. You do not have to respond to the whole piece: it will reveal itself in its entirety in time – that is what the weeks of work with your actors and collaborators are for – but if an image from it sears itself into your mind, if your heart turns over at the thought of a certain line being uttered on the stage, if you know in your bones just how a scene should flow, then invest your time and your energy in the play. Prepare a workbook – and I will discuss how to do that – and start the long labour of finding somewhere to put the play on, and colleagues to labour with you.

You would do well to make a list of every play you can remember seeing and every play you have read. Look at where the gaps are – where there are no Restoration plays or only one Greek tragedy, only a few Shakespeares or wise-cracking American comedies. Then you can begin to direct your reading more efficiently, begin to fill in some of the blank spaces and find the many different sort of plays, comic or tragic, old or new, naturalistic or epic, that stimulate your imagination and make your heart beat faster. And of course, as time goes on, you will find that your tastes change, develop and diversify. Always be updating your list. Life itself will drive you to an artist's work if it helps you to express something of what you have undergone, understand what you have witnessed first hand or empathize with what you see others undergo.

Throughout your directing life you will fall in love with certain plays and keep them on a 'someday to do' list. And a warning – falling in love is painful if you do not get to possess the beloved. When a rarely performed play is directed by someone else, you have to reluctantly move it to the back burner for you know no-one will be willing to mount another production for some years. But still you will have the list and your personal vision of the play and will be waiting for the moment when it can come to life in your hands whether you are twenty-nine or ninety.

It is essential though that you steadily add to your list of 'must do's for you never know when someone will ask you what play you might want to direct. Then you will be ready with some choices. But you do have to be realistic. A theatre with a small space and a tiny budget will not be interested if you declare your true love to be an obscure five-hour epic with fifty characters. It will be outside their scope. There again: obscure they might accept, if you can argue its acute relevance; epic, if you can show how you can use the small space imaginatively; fifty characters if you can show how brilliantly it could be done not by fifty but by five consummate actors – two of whom you already know of and can interest in the project … .

So as you find the plays you want to do, think also of the best kind of spaces for them. Calculate their cast sizes and the rehearsal period you might need, what collaborators you might wish to employ – for music, movement, fights and so on, how complicated a design might be involved. All these will have a bearing on whether a theatre might be willing to help you stage your production. Also think about the kind of actors a play might demand. It is no good trying to do a comedy unless you have in mind or in reality, actors who are naturally gifted, or 'have it for nothing' as you could say of actors who are simply vulnerable, lightning fast or funny because they seem just born that way. It is no good doing a musical unless you have the singers for it, or a commedia piece unless you have the actors mobile enough for it. Think practically.

If you go to someone to pitch the idea for a play, prepare yourself beforehand. Anticipate the questions they might ask. Why this play? How do you imagine it? Have your answers ready. Do not tell them what you think they might want to hear in a vain effort to please. Be sincere and express your personal feelings, your unique response to the piece. Always prepare a single piece of typed foolscap on which you have written a simple outline of your idea, with cast numbers and other relevant details – rehearsal period required, costume demands, set, music, possible collaborators. Leave this with them as you go. This will be a simple reminder of the meeting and one they can use to present your idea to their colleagues.

You might ask yourself or be asked whether a play will be a box-office success. This is the way to madness. No-one can really ever predict what an audience will like, will pay money to see. And to direct a play thinking of only pleasing an audience will put you on the high road to failure. You can only think: Does it make sense to me? Is it moving to me? Does it make me laugh? After all, your putative audience is a fantasy until you take the play into preview. You will alter things then because the audience needs more clarity or because you understand suddenly how the theatricality of a moment can work better. Apart from that, the only person you can seek to please and satisfy is yourself.

There is no predicting box-office. Choose plays because you love them.

6

READING THE PLAY

When I started directing, I put away my actor's make-up one Saturday night at the Citizens Theatre, Glasgow and arrived in the rehearsal room next Monday morning as a director. I had hardly directed so much as a scene before and now the design was in a model box, the workshops downstairs were busy building the set and an opening night was advertised for three and a half weeks hence. It was like being firmly locked inside a hurtling, run-away train.

On the eve of the first rehearsal, I had a nightmare. I was in a room with a mass of actors – I somehow knew there were 200 of them – and I had no idea what to do. So I told them to divide into two groups: one of a hundred people, one of ninety-nine. I pointed to one actor and said, 'You walk straight downstage between them.' The groups formed, the actor stepped forwards. Then he hesitated and said, 'Why?' At that moment, thank God, I woke up.

Brecht's designer and collaborator Caspar Neher kept 'werkbuchen' or workbooks full of vivid drawings and scribblings – settings, moments from an imaginary staging, character sketches. When I came to look at Neher's work, what excited me most were his drawings of scenes that weren't actually in the plays – unwritten meetings, un-staged journeys, un-shown conflicts. I started to amass workbooks in which I not only sank myself deeply into the text, but also wandered imaginatively in and around the world of the play, uncensored, letting my mind meander within its contours.[1]

Your main aim when you start a workbook is to untangle the matted skein of different thoughts and theories you may have after a preliminary reading of a play and allay the anxiety of how to get to grips with it all. You want firstly a workaday, practical method of assimilating and understanding text, always remembering not to preclude what might evolve when you, the actors and the creative team all work together in the rehearsal space. You should avoid definitely deciding things. Let ideas swim vaguely across the page in shorthand notes, scribbled phrases and rough drawings. In other words, aim not to plan but to prepare; find starting points, not results.

- Do not use the book to make final decisions about the particulars of staging.
- Do not use the book to predict actors' activities.
- Do not use the book to dictate actors' choices.

I begin by equipping myself with a fresh new notebook – part of my ritual is to choose the blank book carefully in a stationery store – for an aesthetic enjoyment of work is important from the very beginning. I collect together pen, coloured pencils, scissors, glue and a ruler. I place the two large volumes of the Oxford English Dictionary on my desk. This shows my age and disposition as I prefer to leaf through the pages rather than Google a word. My lap-top, though, is indispensible for research. I work at a desk, not lolling on a sofa with the play in my hand – that leads only to thoughts of cups of tea, bars of chocolate and urgent phone calls to make.

If you work at a desk with a pencil in your hand, you will not be subject to vague impressions but methodical examination of the text. The text is God. If a director cannot find justification in the text, there is no justification. Find out what the writer is trying to tell you before you set yourself up as better than the writer. Otherwise, you will be subject to that bane of a director's life – the good idea without proper foundation in the text. This is often catastrophic because the misguided director spends masses of energy bending the play to fit in with a theory of it, and the world ends up with superficial updatings, spurious versions and monstrous distortions of plays that do not illuminate them but merely force them into a construct of the director's making. You can hardly find an opera nowadays which is not re-set in a car warehouse, a skating rink or some other arbitrary space. I am reminded of James Fenton's remark when watching an updated classical play. He felt that had the actors not been dressed as members of the German revolutionary group, Baader Meinhof, the play might have powerfully reminded him of ... the Baader Meinhof Group.[2]

I work methodically at a desk like this because I have always found simply reading through a play again and again rather confusing. I tend at first reading to skim through it, getting only a rough sense of it. In fact, a play almost gives off a scent for me and I soon know if I am getting the wrong odour from it. With a bad play, I can hardly turn the pages over after the first scene or two. With one that excites me I read almost without a pause. But always when I come to properly digest the written word, I need to annotate and make notes and lists. And because a play is not writing but talking, I always feel it must be read aloud. It is good to get the words in your ears and in your mouth – not so that you can make a decision as to how they will be spoken, but so that you begin to grasp them with your senses as well as your intellect, because acting and directing is above all a sensuous process. It is not theoretical but practical. It happens through bodies and minds in the space, not as a construct in the director's head. So I speak it very quietly, almost unvoiced – I do not want to become too attached to my particular reading of a line – and let the shape of the words roll through my mouth.

I work with a dictionary because it is important, especially in an old play, that you find how the meanings of words have changed over time. They are often listed in the dictionary together with a date. You think you might know, but it is often a revelation to find the original meaning of a word, or how meaning has evolved over time. Just think of the changes the word 'gay' has undergone in the last fifty years, or 'neat' in American. Now the words 'fit' and 'allow' are shape-shifting in my daughter's London speech.[3]

On the first page of the notebook, I leave a large gap and then I write the title of the play and the name of the playwright. This is my first building block and I go on from there to construct a very big edifice indeed. Turning over the page, I note the writer's dates and the date the play was written and then I find the political, social and cultural events that surround these dates and anything of biographical interest that might seem to have some bearing on the play. When I first started making workbooks, I found one day in a second-hand bookshop a volume called *The Chronology of World History* in three volumes and this has been invaluable to me. This gives me the paintings, the books, the scientific discoveries, the political events, notable births and deaths carefully listed for every year from 1600 to 1900.[4] From this, I can find among many other fascinating facts, what postcards of paintings to prop up on my desk and what music to listen to while I am preparing a production.

But most importantly at the beginning of my workbook, I look up in the dictionary every word of the title. Of course, if it consists of a single name – Macbeth or Coriolanus – this may not yield much you do not already know, but on one occasion the first pages of a workbook led me to change my mind almost completely about my reluctance to direct Shakespeare's *The Taming of the Shrew*. In 1983, I had been to a particularly frustrating interview at the Royal Shakespeare Company in London where I had been urged to consider directing *As You Like It* or *The Taming of the Shrew* – plays which I considered 'girls' choices and was therefore opposed to doing at this early point in my career. In fact, I thought *The Taming of the Shrew* could only be authentically played as a thoroughly misogynist piece of work. Once home, though, I started a couple of workbooks and looking up the word 'shrew' in the dictionary discovered that the shrew, a mammal with a small stomach and a voracious appetite is constantly hungry and as a result emits high-pitched sounds of distress. This sound gave rise to the association with the high pitch of a woman's complaining voice. I suddenly began to see Katherine in a new light: motherless and hungry for attention, offered like a commodity in marriage to a self-confessed fortune-hunter, she expresses through the only weapon she has to hand – shrewishness – her inner pain. I then knew I wanted to direct the play. And all this from researching one word.

The title of the play analysed, look at the writer's life and times. At what point in their lives was the play written? What was happening in their world? At what point in history did they set the play? Why? What aspects of the writer's life could throw some light onto the subject matter of the play?

Then turn to the body of the text. Look for indications of the location: where it is set. Look not only at the literal setting but what that might mean for the writer in his time. What did Venice mean for Shakespeare or the Italian court of Malfi for Webster or Sidcup for Harold Pinter? Begin on a separate page or in different-coloured ink or pencil, topics for research. These locations are probably going to be your first research topics and so leave plenty of room to fill these in later. For the moment go on reading the text aloud. Then, pencil in hand, mark where you consider the main sections of the text fall – number these and give them each a simple one-sentence description which will guide you through the bare bones of the story. This is what I wrote when first preparing the opera *Gawain*.

GAWAIN – section breakdown:
SECTION 1. Morgan Le Fay appears from the ether – she cannot be seen although we can see her.
SECTION 2. The court of King Arthur assembles.
SECTION 3. The King will not join the knights and Guinevere at the table.

Leave a space for each section and then go back and fill in the details of the physical environment – the time, season, weather and any particular details of setting the text alludes to – a tree, a stove, a rock, a door, a bed.

GAWAIN – section breakdown:
1. Morgan Le Fay appears from the ether. She cannot be seen by the court.
winter,
snow,
night,
Christmas in the human world, she is in another world
magic – how to suggest it?
costume – winter: fur? warriors?
what exactly is a Fool?

2. The court of King Arthur assembles.
winter,
night,
snow outside,
wind howling,
mass of Christ's birth early Christian festival, consisting of what?
feast – is there food? getting food on and off / eating and singing
ritual attendance of the knights at the royal court – how do they assemble?

3. The King will not join the knights and Guinevere at the table.
Inner space – Morgan can enter and be invisible at will – how to suggest it?
Hall of a castle – cold primitive stone – how suggested?
Round table readied for feast – getting round table on and off? When knights sit and king not, sit on what?

When this is all done, you can draw for yourself a crazy, imaginary map of houses and gardens, hills and battlefields, shrines and government offices alluded to in your text. You can work out where the babies sleep in *The Three Sisters*, where the guests at a banquet have dined in *Macbeth*, where the secret door to the bedchamber might be in *The Duchess of Malfi*. These are not fixed in stone and can constantly change as you read on but they will give you the edifices and landscape beyond and behind the action played on the stage.

This off-stage landscape will develop in the work the actors do in the rehearsal room and affect subtly their body language in the stage space, as they turn their heads towards unseen rooms, shrink from the sound of distant battlefields or fantasize about Sidcup. You will find it useful to practise a bit of drawing – understanding how to render perspective and to draw simple figures. Take a look at maps drawn for readers of history books or those wonderful maps which evoke childhood landscapes or the domain of hobbits. Directing students at the Drama Centre did drawing lessons each week, not for skill in drawing per se but so that they could feel more expressive in their own workbooks. Caspar Neher often drew scenes that did not actually occur in the play – scenes that were referred to or scenes he simply imagined – and you can do this too.

Now you can go back over the text again – this will be your third or fourth time – and start to investigate the characters. You could try to glean from the text family trees and inter-relationships by marriage. Next put aside a few pages per character (more for the major ones) and divide the pages into two columns: in one you will write phrases from the text where the characters describe themselves and in the other, phrases used by others to describe them. A quick look down these lists will evoke a vivid image of each character and you will be able to note characters' ages, professions, physical characteristics and emotional tendencies. These will provide you with other topics to jot down on your research list. You may notice a new reference to the time or the weather and you can add to the notes you have made about physical environment.

Your list of research topics will start to grow and you will tackle each of these later. What you should be deeply aware of is that characteristics reveal themselves slowly throughout the action. You may find you will now sometimes adjust your diagram of the family tree, marking in a different colour underlying alliances or antipathies. Writing phrases from the text laboriously in long hand also means the play sinks right into your mind and you will not have to constantly refer to it in the rehearsal room.

Go through the text yet again. You are now looking at the social environment of the play: what cosmological beliefs apply, what religious concepts, what social rules, what manners, what etiquette? What beliefs about sexual morals prevail, about integrity in business, obedience to the King, faithfulness to a spouse? How far do these belief structures control the different characters? Is there a prevalent belief in a Christian concept of God? Do all the characters share this belief or only some? Is the King there by Divine Right? Will there be a judgement after death? Is love caused by the arbitrary shot of an arrow from a blind boy flying around the sky? This is where the world of the theatre and the world of anthropology most nearly collide for me. Making a workbook becomes like studying a primitive tribe, turning the culture of the play under my gaze like a prism to see what belief worlds the characters inhabit.

You may by now have spent days in work but trawl the text yet again – mainly, but not necessarily, the beginning scenes, and look for events alluded to in the text but which happened before the action of the play began. In movie terms, this is going to give you a lot of back stories – experiences the characters have undergone before the action of the play begins. I use these later as the basis of much of my early semi-improvisational work in the rehearsal room when I devise scenarios which will lead the actors from previous experiences towards a phrase or reference in the text.

You should also note characters who are alluded to in the text but who do not actually appear in the play. These shadowy off-stage characters can provide you with staging ideas which are based firmly in the text. In Shakespeare's *As You Like It*, there are several textual references to the off-stage figure of a friar. To aid my scene changes I used this figure of a friar wandering the Forest of Arden as a kind of St Francis, begging for alms. Although only glancingly referred to as an off-stage character in the actual text, I also used him to officiate at the weddings in the last act. When Jaques declared at the end of the play that he was off to join the friar in the religious life, the audience knew him well as a character. Similarly, in *The Duchess of Malfi*, the Cardinal mentions that the ghost 'of an old woman, which is given/By tradition to us to have been murder'd/By her nephews, for her riches' haunts his brother. This image of a group of ghostly victims, joined in the fifth act by the Duchess herself, is woven through the whole production and, by the way, solves one of the so-called problems of the play – that the Duchess disappears before the final act. Her ghost does not.

Finally, you should look carefully at the structure of the play. Does it move in a straight line through time? Is there direct audience address? Is there a narrator? Is there a chorus?

When for instance, I looked at the structure of *The Taming of the Shrew*, I did not recognize the play I thought I knew. Here was an opening scene of a beggar being thrown out of an ale house and sinking into a drunken sleep on the streets. Then I saw I was looking at a prologue. *The Taming of the Shrew*, as we see it for the main part in performance, is in fact written as a play within a play in which some players perform for a beggar as part of a trick to convince him he is actually a rich man. Then as I proceeded with my workbook I found the actors' play described by Shakespeare as a 'kind of history': and I saw that this story of Katherine's capitulation was a history and not a herstory.[5] Thus. with no distortion of the text, by use of simple images, the inner play could be held up for examination as a kind of history, but not the only history. The prologue or outer play concerned a trick being played upon our drunken tramp. He would awake a rich man, having a play performed for him. He would even have the promise of a beautiful wife. When, the play over, the trick was finally revealed and he was returned to his beggarly state, the leading actress – a hardworking mother of a young baby – would also be returned to her real state. It would be the drunken beggar and the woman sweeping the stage after the performance (who, acting a part, had seemed so happy as Katherine to put her hand under her husband's foot), who would be revealed as those at the bottom of history's heap.

You will now have the text of the play really under your belt. You will be able to scan your lists to make a breakdown for a casting director. You will know (without in any way dictating what the design should be) what the play demands from its design. You may have a sense of the vital turns in the narrative that will give the play pace and excitement. You will know what facts the audience have to understand to follow the narrative and in which lines precisely this information resides. You will understand through what devices the story is told. In short, you now have in the workbook a basis for a putative production.

Over the next days and weeks, you will find yourself constantly thinking of the play, and all kinds of stray information you encounter will have a bearing upon it – you may find a newspaper cutting, a photograph, a painting which elucidates a moment within it. Paste images like these into the book. Images of costumes or hairstyles, swathes of colour, swatches of material – all these can go into the workbook and power up your imagination and help to elucidate your ideas. You do not have to be too literal about them: an image might evoke a light or a shadow or an atmosphere that seems relevant.

In *Gawain*, I was much pre-occupied by the notion of ritual. The composer, Birtwistle, had written a most elaborate masque to end the first act, in which during the passing of the seasons of the year, day and night, and the phases of the moon, the pieces of Gawain's armour were ritually strapped to him. In 1990, deep into my work on the opera, I visited Chartres cathedral. It was cold weather in the north of France and my baby was bundled up in a fur-lined hat and coat. When walking with her down the aisle of the cathedral, I noticed an intricate pattern on the floor. It was a medieval labyrinth, built around 1200 and meant to be walked – sometimes it was even danced – as a symbolic pilgrimage to Jerusalem, and as a result came to be called the 'chemin de Jerusalem' or way to Jerusalem. In walking the labyrinth the pilgrim travels through each of the four quadrants of a circle several times before reaching the goal. An observer looking not at the floor but from a distance at the moving figures, cannot imagine when or how the centre will be reached. I looked at my daughter bundled up in her fur-lined hat, and down at the labyrinth, and suddenly the entire ritual of the masque fell into my mind complete. Against the winter cold, the knights could be wrapped in primitive heavy fur-lined cloaks (anything to avoid the cliché of wrinkly tights and knitted metal tabards) and their ritual arming might involve walking a complex pavement maze towards the central figure of Gawain.

Returning to London, where a similar maze had just been revealed on the floor of Westminster Abbey, I started to look in workshop at other geometrical shapes and found the pentangle – referred to in the original poem of Gawain as an ancient shape used in spells and incantation – which at the intersection of the lines of its five points describes a circle. Alison Chitty, the designer, came up with the idea of a great round stone table which sank into a floor in which parts of the pentangle were etched in silver. Further concentric circles gave the masque its outer spaces for the movements of the moon and the seasons, with a beautiful arc drawn from the medieval book of hours, *Les Très Riches Heures du Duc de Berry*, dominating the enactment of the masque. Thus many disparate discoveries and reveries flowed into the final stage image.

At the end of all this methodical labour, you have a workbook filled with lists, notes and cuttings that give you the world of the play. You could take it with you into rehearsal and show the actors all the work you have done; you could use it as a basis for your first day's brilliant talk on the play and your production concept. But you do nothing of that sort. You turn back to the first page and write down in the gap you left as you started the book, Brecht's phrase, 'work makes you confident' and then you put the book on your bookshelf and go to rehearsals ready, not to look in a book, but to follow your instincts from what you experience in front of your eyes.

7

CASTING THE PLAY

A fisherman casts a net into the sea and hauls up fish: you can see how the word came into the theatre. Casting brings with it a sense of trawling, of throwing out a line with the bait of a part. And when one day I saw one of those vast open casting calls in a New York studio with a hundred people waiting in line to get two minutes in front of director and producer, my heart quailed at the sight. They were like so many flopping fish gasping for air. First and foremost, look at the casting process from the actors' point of view. The call for an audition is the first point of contact the actor has with that most elusive of experiences: a job. An audition comes brimming with promise and fantasy. To properly prepare for an audition the actor must throw himself imaginatively into the part he hopes to play, the words he might be called upon to read, the speech he has been preparing. The morning of an audition is a morning with purpose, with shape, with hope – in a life spent mainly doing things the actor wasn't trained for and doesn't much like. Often the whole week is lit up by the audition. 'I'm going up for a job on Wednesday', the actor says delightedly.

An actor worth his salt prepares. The hair is washed, the clothes chosen: all is expectation. The very least a director can do is to have the imagination to empathize a little with what emotions and preparations lie behind the actor's entry into a room with a script in his hand. And in the American theatre it is often not even a script but a tiny portion of it: sides or pages. So actors often do not even have an overview of the part they prepare for, merely some text on a page or two, as if to emphasize their marginality in the enterprise.

In the age of print and computers, you should treat the actors with the respect they deserve and furnish them with the whole play. No matter how small a part you may be asking them to play, anyone with a real understanding of what makes a play work knows that every cog in the machine matters. Where, for instance, would we be in *Twelfth Night* if the Sea Captain in the first scene did not deliver with vivid clarity his recollection of the storm which has brought Viola to the shore but has cast Sebastian upon the sea? The actor and the director are engaged in a complex courtship ritual: young unknown actors wooing the director, for make no mistake the actor is doing something most people dread. They are asking someone to love them and often the answer is no. Rejection is always painful. Later the power relationship can change. The director sometimes woos the actor. An actor of a certain standing and repute is often offended if asked to read for a part, the underlying assumption being that you must have seen them work, you know their skill and they need not, indeed cannot properly, demonstrate it by something as superficial as a reading. What is being decided is: will the production be worth the actor's time and energy? Will he enjoy the play and this particular director's rehearsal process? And between these two scenarios lie complex and subtle variations in the power relationship, between who represents at any moment the wooer and the wooed.

With older actors who are not particularly well known, bringing into the room with them perhaps forty years or more of struggle and survival, a director should be aware of how much it means to their pride and dignity for an audition to proceed as if they were not the wooer, when in fact they are. Many directors do not for one moment examine their quiet enjoyment of power, and in the casting process they give full rein to this pathetic lack of self-awareness. Never fall into the trap of not being on the side of the actor, and remind yourself often that you are only one part of a shared endeavour.

At the base of the casting process is the director's need to find the actor who will bring real creativity to the process and this is not just a question of acting talent. What you are looking for is the actor's potential in three areas:

- The ability, with proper rehearsal, to embody the character
- The ability to work in a way that enables the director to be creative
- The ability to form part of the company the director is creating.

There are many talented actors capable of playing each part. The bottom line is: do you want this person around for weeks on end and at moments when you might all come up against difficulties and disagreements? Casting directors are sensitive not only to the right actor for the part but also for the right personality match between actor and director.

You must also be careful when casting plays or characters which demand very particular skills. I was warned as a young director of those plays where everything depends upon casting. Notoriously, you cannot do a comedy without actors who are just naturally funny, or complex text without actors who have vocal skill in bringing out complex thought, or a play in a big theatre with an actor who has a limited voice or not enough stamina.

A good casting director talks of an actor's inner reserves of pain, demons or emotional volts. Some actors can just access certain emotions or play a vulnerability as if born to it. Others can only impersonate it; some actors live it. Only experience will show you when such actors have to be sought. On the other hand, try to avoid closed thinking about appearances. Nothing, for instance, saps an actress of her off-stage beauty as much as a lack of sheer talent. Her beauty will simply evaporate on stage if she has not the wherewithal to play the part well. Some actresses, altogether rather ordinary off-stage, can become ineffably beautiful if they are in marvellous free flow in a role. There is something touching and thrilling about an actress who un-made-up, tired and weather-beaten, enters a theatre by the stage door at the end of a busy day and two hours later moves you to tears by her sheer translucent beauty of face and spirit. In fact the very capability to transform emotionally and physically is a major part of any actor's brilliance.

In this area there is a distinct difference between the European and American casting cultures, perhaps because of the American emphasis on screen acting where an actor's appearance takes precedence over much else. English actors are always told they should dress especially smartly for American directors and producers. What they consider attractive differs from European standards and most certainly English ones, where self-effacement is the norm. Actresses are advised to wear clothes that show off their figures and to put on make-up. Actresses in Los Angeles often appear for auditions in teetering heels and tight dresses, whereas in London a much more casual and everyday look, erring much more on the side of grunge, is completely acceptable.

Beneath these outward and seemingly minor indicators lie deeper assumptions. I believe European actors are workaday because of their belief that they are creatures capable of transformation: that is their work, their art form, their métier. They are not simply their appearance. 'You will get much more than you first see,' is what the actor seems to say: the more ordinary their everyday appearance, the more starling their transformation. English actors do not give everything away at once. They are often rather subdued and self-effacing. They do not present themselves as showmen and they are unwilling merchants in the market place. And it is the notion of the market that separates the two cultures. American actors are encouraged to unselfconsciously sell themselves, to be gracious, grateful, pleasing – to deliver from the outset something near their finished performance. There is money, investment of capital riding on their showmanship. European actors forged in a much longer and more soundly theatrical rather than movie tradition, bring something of the pride of their long and not ignoble history with them. Their art, they seem to imply, is in the becoming. They show you a potential, not a finished, product. American actors often feel forced to come up with a choice, practised and polished. The drawback is that rehearsal sometimes does not move them on in the way it can in Europe where the process not the result is more honoured. The notion of slow food is here the simple analogy. Good ingredients, prepared slowly, will taste better than fast food that looks superficially attractive.

Actors in this market-place atmosphere are expected to be pleasing – and above all quick at it. So American students are often told by their teachers that they must stand and deliver a speech in an audition without any delay. Actors feel they can take no time to prepare and rarely put on a practice skirt or a pair of suitable shoes. The underlying assumption is that they are to do their thing and get out of the room as quickly as possible: that a swift and efficient judgement will be made in a matter of minutes. Actors are timetabled every five or ten minutes. It is as if the vast department stores with endless choice of goods or the infinite varieties of coffee on sale at every corner have translated into an audition situation which is measured for efficiency by quantity and through-put.

My advice to any director is to err on the side of attention to detail, to give yourself and the actor time to breathe and get a sense of each other. I bring actors into auditions at a rate of three or four an hour. You may have to spend time with people you sense almost immediately are not what you are looking for, but on balance it is better to see fewer actors for longer in any day and try to get some proper measure of their potential.

Beware of the casting cliché: wives are not invariably suburban or homely; doctors are not necessarily serious, wise or sober; vicars come young, long-haired and gay; soldiers can be nervous and puny; prostitutes do not wiggle their hips or show a startling cleavage: they are too often waiting for a fix and shivering in a thin jacket on a cold night. There are many clichés in casting. Avoid them: think laterally.

Give some thought to how you arrange a room where you audition. Make sure there are seats somewhere outside for the actors to wait. Try hard to keep on time. Burned in my memory is an audition I had once at a

London theatre when John Osborne and his director (thankfully his name eludes my memory) kept me waiting for over an hour and then rolled in from a boozy lunch talking about the champagne they had drunk. I had borrowed my tube fare to get there.

Order the room so that it is not intimidating from the actor's point of view. Place the chairs in a non-confrontational position and keep lists of actors and piles of photographs and CVs out of sight. We all know every part is fought over; there is no need to rub the actor's nose in it. Do not make written notes when the actor is in the room. Wait until they have left. Introduce anyone auditioning with you – be it an assistant, casting director or colleague – by their full name and get them to stand up and shake hands. Stand up yourself as the actor enters and reach out your hand. If you are in a theatre, make your way to the stage – do not loll in the stalls calling out from the darkness like some oriental pasha. Avoid all such forms of de-personalization.

Read the actor's CV or resumé before they come in, looking for some point of contact – a play you have seen them in, a director they have worked for, a play you both might know, who recommended them to you and why: all this serves to put the actor at ease and gives you a chance to exercise your intuition about them. Concentrate only on them – their emotional weight and volume as they walk across the room – nothing to do with their actual weight and height but how they inhabit the space. Note the minutiae of body language. When actors read, try to give them some alternative choices – suggest different actions or another way into the scene – and note how receptive they are to notes, their capacity to imaginatively change. Talk a little about their lives: all the time gauging how they score in the three criteria you have set.

It is always indicative if the actor has not read the play. Sometimes truthfully it arrived at the last moment, or they have been working or otherwise busy, but serious actors will nearly always have read the play and be ready to talk about their feelings about it even if their major feeling is that they want to be acting, for God's sake, in this or any other play. A lack of preparation for an audition is often a sign that actors are disheartened with the whole process and are somehow avoiding the pang of rejection in advance by pretending to themselves they did not want the part anyway, that they did not prepare adequately for it and therefore cannot be judged.

In advising actors on how to tackle auditioning, I always suggest that they keep a journal and give each director they meet a score out of ten for their demeanour and their ability to get the best out of an actor, for their ability to conduct an audition well is a sign of how well they might run rehearsals. It is salutary to remember that the actor, no matter how obscure, may also be auditioning you.

As a preparation for auditioning it is useful to prepare a casting breakdown: the details on character should come from the text or good research. This breakdown can go to a casting director or an assistant, can help you when asking friends or colleagues for ideas and can force you to think clearly as to your needs. If you have to find actors to double parts, list what possible combinations could work but keep an open mind. In my experience the possible double arrives with the actual actor whom you suddenly see can play, in a way you had never imagined, contrasting roles to perfection.

Here is an example of a casting breakdown I sent to Serena Hill, the casting director at the National Theatre in London when I was preparing *Remembrance of Things Past*. This was a play Harold Pinter and I adapted from Marcel Proust's novel *À La Recherche du Temps Perdu*. It required actors who would respond with enthusiasm to the particular demands of the script, where with three exceptions there were no leading parts and the actors needed to really embrace the notion of doubling and have the capacity to play across a whole spectrum of the classes and the minutiae of social differences that Proust so vividly and comically dissects.

Marcel: first seen as a child, half-Jewish narrator, bookends the play as a dying man in his first appearance, but his major scenes feature him in his obsessive love affair with Albertine as a young man, youngish pretty boy of letters, beautiful eyes.

Mother: modelled on Proust's Jewish mother whom he adored, as she was when he was a child and young man, haute bourgeoise doctor's wife 40? doubling.[1]

Father: strict and conventional father moving in middle-class society, as a doctor, country neighbour to Swann to whom he is patronizing, narrow-minded, could later double as part of the Verdurin set.

Grandmother: kindly, patient, adoring, failing during the course of the play 60–70–80? slightly dotty.

Swann: one of Proust's great creations; half-Jewish, impeccably courteous country neighbour to Marcel's family who look down on him because of his marriage. His obsessive love for the demi-mondaine Odette pre-dates Marcel's agony with Albertine by a generation, never lets on to those who are snobbish towards him that he has moved in the very best of circles – member of the Jockey Club, friend of the Prince of Wales. A complete gentleman, impeccably dressed (hats lined with green leather), accomplished, graceful, doomed.

Duchesse de Guermantes: adored from afar by Marcel as a child, the epitome of aristocratic elegance. Fair hair, periwinkle blue eye, Fortuny gowns.

Duc de Guermantes: monocle, dark, gleaming teeth, famous for the moment when on hearing from Swann that he is mortally ill, responds by sending his wife upstairs to change her shoes to match her dress.

Rachel: famous actress, attractive on stage, plain close to, tragedian, mistress among others of St Loup, accepted by society because of her talent (Rejane).

Odette: modelled among others on Liane de Pougy, famous demi-mondaine. Very beautiful vacuous young woman with whom Swann falls in love and commits social suicide by marrying, has a fantastic scene where she admits her lesbian infidelities to Swann.

Madame Verdurin: fat, breathless, henna'd hair, excessively rich and socially undistinguished, it is at her instigation that Morel publically humiliates Charlus.

Baron de Charlus: Grand Duke of Sodom, one of Proust's great creations, modelled on Robert de Montesquiou, allied, as he never tires of saying, to the greater part of European aristocracy. Languorous, high-pitched voice, refined hybrid creature, a voracious pursuer of rough trade – footmen, soldiers, the boy who sells chestnuts on the corner. Plump shuffling old man at the final reception, we see him mainly at his most virulently outrageous, great scene is when he is humiliated publically by his protégé Morel and is rescued by his cousin, the Queen of Naples.

Albertine: one of the band of young girls with whom Marcel falls obsessively in love, boyish perhaps, pretty, beguiling, has perhaps a secret bisexual life – we never know for certain. The young Colette.

A list such as this, drawn from a carefully researched workbook, can give you and your colleagues some idea of the task in hand. After all you have to live with your casting choices through rehearsal and into the run of the play. This is why directors are often in throes of indecision or desperate when particular actors turn them down. Your casting will always be a compromise between fantasy and reality but at least by giving the process time, thought and a certain amount of dignity, you can better live with your choices – and then there is always the glorious actor who repays your gamble in spades and reminds you of why you loved the theatre in the first place.

8

REHEARSING THE ACTORS

Managing time

Acting is a mystery. I do not know precisely how it all happens in the rehearsal room. I am only grateful that it does. One day the actors are slogging workman-like through lines, trying first one idea and then another. Without warning something changes – a quality, an atmosphere, an echo in the memory. These moments of breakthrough, of intuition, of clashing temperament and easy laughter are indefinable and at the core of the rehearsal experience, and the time it takes to happen – if indeed it does happen – is entirely unpredictable. What unlocks good acting is as various as actors themselves. And the longer you work with actors, the more careful you become with generalizations. This is part of the excitement and fascination with directing – the more you do it the less you know for certain how it happens or why it happens when it does. You can only comfort yourself with the thought that you have done plays before so you will no doubt do this one too.

Work with every new actor is the work of getting to know another human being and earning a sort of trust. It is easy in a sense since actors rely on a good director – the outside eye – to guide the building of a performance, but once you make actors distrust your judgement, they will close themselves down in self-defence. After all they are the ones who have to go out there and face an audience in a matter of weeks. If they begin to think that what you say or propose will stop them working freely altogether, you will become powerless. If you are lucky they will tolerate but ignore you; if unlucky they will resort to any ploy to shut you out of what they can salvage from their creative process. And a group of actors intent on saving their skins can turn into a wolf-pack. A group can become toxic.

Above all else acting is a sensuous process. It happens through the muscle and the heart and the intestines, it moves through the body and the intangibles of fantasy, imagination and the subconscious. You do acting by the act – you cannot think, plan or talk it into existence. You cannot predict the time it will take. So above all else allow actors to keep acting. That is what the term rehearse means – going over something again and again but with the minutest of changing inflexions and intentions, with ideas and suggestions feeding in, until something seamless and altogether effortless is built.

To get there takes time and sweat and above all, patience. You should never therefore harry the actor early in rehearsal to embody characteristics only revealed later in the text or expect an actor to bring forth a fully formed character as he slowly works his way into the play. You might have an image in your mind. Through your preparation, your deep knowledge of the text you may be ahead of him in the game. Essentially, your image of the character is just that – an image, a notion, a chimera. Only the actor can embody it and bring it into existence. You can talk about it, you might possibly be able to write an academic thesis on the play and the function of this character within it, but you are not going to live it or breathe it or dance it or laugh it.

You are not the creator. You can guide the construct, but it will never be your creation – your muscle will not go into it. Bide your time. Trying to get the actor to come fully formed as a character too soon in the process is one of the worst faults of inexperienced directors. The actor can only play moment to moment what the text allows him, and can only go at the pace of his own, as it were, muscular discovery. If late in the play, some realization brings the character to transformation, to profound change in attitude, the actor will be intent on only gradually revealing this. He might alternatively find a key physical or emotional characteristic late in the rehearsal period. All this will take time. In a deep sense, you will be powerless.

Rehearsing involves repetition of the text but this should never become mechanical. There is nothing more deadening and frustrating for an actor than to trawl through a scene again and again in the same way knowing that there is something fundamentally wrong or inadequate in it. 'All we do is run it', they complain to each other. And they are quite right to do so.

A scene or section may well be superficially adequate in that it proceeds in some kind of believable shape. The poor directors may be happy to leave it at that because at base, their major sensation has nothing to do with what is going on in the room, in front of their eyes. Their major sensation is anxiety: anxiety about what they are going to have come up with three, four, or five weeks hence. They cannot be fully in the process because they are already too worried about what the eventual result will be. Anxiety is the antithesis of creativity. Worried directors may look at a scene and think with relief, 'This at least is presentable. I will have something to show an audience.' They may be content to leave it at that. And the actors become adept at repeating superficiality. Underneath they agonize and seethe. They know a better scene is inside there somewhere and the rehearsal process is not allowing them to try to get at it, to re-think, to try other tactics. The director is wasting time. Find a way to leave anxiety at the door of the rehearsal room. A painstaking re-examination of all the factors in a scene for more and more discoveries is part of the empiric process of play-making, and work can reveal quite astonishing unimagined possibilities. And the mosaic which is the rehearsal process shifts not only in space but also in time.

Calls

Remember you have to both forget the clock and be controlled by it. So do not bring a rehearsal to an end for the sake of punctuality when you feel on the verge of a breakthrough. And try always to leave the actors at the end of a rehearsal session with a feeling of having edged forward, solved some of the task. Always allow them time to go over the work of the session so that it settles in their muscles and their senses: this will requires a period of time set aside simply for working through without the director interrupting. On the other hand, so over-running your calls that the next actors are kept interminably waiting to work saps their goodwill and energy.

Once you have decided when calls with the actors should begin and end, you can slot in meetings with other members of your team. Make sure you do not fit into an unsuitable timetable just because it is the convention. I, for instance, prefer to have early morning meetings outside rehearsals – tough on a technician working a show the night before, but otherwise the director gets no break in the middle of the day and spends lunchtimes gulping food and fielding questions, usually without quite enough thought. You have to have time to say 'I don't know yet' and send someone away without an answer – as important as coming up with a quick answer.

Give some thought too to your potential level of fatigue. When I had a young child waking eagerly at 5:30 each morning, I directed a production at the National Theatre and an opera at Covent Garden. I called a one and a half hour break for lunch, slept for one hour in an empty dressing room, ate a sandwich which was left there for me at two o'clock, washed my face in cold water and went back to work again. My daughter, taken in her pushchair to see me when I was rehearsing at Covent Garden, pointed to the opera house and told her nanny, 'That's an opera house', and added informatively, 'It's where my mother lives.' In Stratford in 1987 when I had a two-month-old baby, I solved the problem by going to bed at 7:30 in the evening and having my nanny slide the carry cot with the sleeping baby in it inside my bedroom door after her ten o'clock evening feed. With luck, she slept until about four in the morning. I then fed her and had a few hours alone with her as the dawn came up. By the time I arrived at rehearsal, I had been awake for six hours. When the production moved into the theatre, I had to leave home for a few days.

I do not know of any theatre that has crèche facilities. I was told early in my career by the National Theatre casting director Gillian Diamond, never to mention the fact that I had children and never to question an arrangement because of domestic difficulties. 'They don't like it,' she said bluntly. It was possible to be a woman director in the early 1980s but it was better to all intents and purposes to be a woman who was just like a man.

All these considerations mean that the task of when to call the actors and what to rehearse from day to day needs a great deal of thought, and the needs of the piece and the actors are ever changing if you are really alive to proper creative work. Too often calls are announced by the stage manager at the end of a rehearsal after a hurried conversation with the director. The actors often linger in the rehearsal room to get the next day's call before they leave, and you can make a hasty and bad decision under this pressure. In the age of text and e-mail when calls are easy to communicate later in the day, the director should always take time to consider carefully what the calls should be. A solo call with an individual before the bulk is rehearsed may save time and energy, as may a rather technical slow-motion mastery of complex activities with props or costume before you turn to the emotional heart of a scene. Then again technical matters cannot be separated from character, emotional intensity or objectives and the director must try to juggle the one with the other to use time well.

If you are working in a busy company situation with actors performing shows in the evening after rehearsal, the latest time they can be released is rigidly and rightly fixed. There may be actors who are not involved in performances and therefore certain scenes which can be looked at late in a rehearsal day, if you can find the energy. In the more arduous world of much fringe work, the actors may well have to leave for money-earning jobs and directors have to juggle time accordingly.

You have to keep an eye on the future too. Stage managers will remind you sometimes late in the day that an actor will not be available on the morrow and this can throw out all your calculations. So give time to your stage manager at the end of the day: they are immensely helpful if they feel you know how important their part of time management is. In opera, calls days or even weeks in advance are sometimes requested. I always try to avoid locking myself into a timetable that has nothing to do with the changing demands of the piece, but sometimes it is inevitable if large numbers of people have to be somehow organized.

It is useful to learn how in a rehearsal process a lot of time can be saved later by giving up a bit of time earlier. This is especially important in the area of costume and props where a director should exercise every bit of charm and pressure to get an actual prop, costume or piece of furniture into the rehearsal room as soon as possible and give up the odd half an hour to the actors getting used to it. No director should be in any doubt that if a scenic feature, a flight of stairs, a ladder, or a lamp-post an actor can lean on, is not in the acting space in rehearsal, it will never be used to its full potential in the production and time spent getting it into the rehearsal space will be doubly compensated for later.

Getting into the space

The empty space of any rehearsal room can be frightening. And for the actor, there is nothing more wretched and inadequate than that first inarticulate step into the taped lines of the set with a script in their hands. But it is important to get your actors up on their feet and into the space as soon as you can. Perhaps it is because I was an actor myself, and a nervous one at that, that I try to take the pressure off actors in the first days of rehearsal. 'No acting necessary' is my slogan. A director might do well to aim to start work without anyone really noticing it has started.

The usual configuration of the rehearsal room is a set of tables for the stage management and director at the front of the acting area. It is a leftover from the framed viewpoint of proscenium stage. As a young actress I always found it unnecessarily hierarchal – a sort of committee room with rehearsing actors struggling in front of staring spectators. Directors often lock themselves into a sort of defended space behind a desk with the bible of the text at the ready before them. I began to notice actors soon found their own little private – you could say defended – spots in a rehearsal room behind furniture or in corners and crannies, like cats about to give birth to kittens, where they would mouth lines, try out shadow movements, or sip tea and just think. And who could blame them?

On the first morning, the company met for the first time. Sometimes a few of them had worked together before and there was a palpable sense of relief when actors saw people they knew. But all is new – new space, new technicians, new project, new challenges. I saw that people put their coats and bags down haphazardly at the front of the room and all kinds of detritus from coffee cups to half-read newspapers soon built up as people chattered nervously on the edge of the rehearsal space. Then there came a moment when everyone sat before the director and the room was magisterially addressed on his – in my days as an actress there was no her – vision of the play. There were star directors in those days who 'talked a play' well. This was usually followed by a showing of the set model and a talk by the designer. There eventually proceeded a nervous reading – the actors sitting in a circle with their scripts in hand accompanied by much mysterious note-taking by onlookers. Some of the actors gave a sort of performance; some simply read the words. There was in those days an unspoken division between an old-school belief among the established actors – forged by years in weekly repertory – that the young mumbled and it was not playing the game to not have a stab at performance, and the younger generation of actors, schooled in Stanislavsky technique, who felt they should take their time. Everything began seated and with the words on the page. And it was exceedingly nerve-wracking, even though I was always one of those actors who threw themselves straight into a role from first reading. Then usually, the director began to block the scenes in a taped mark-up of the set as the actors moved around, script in hand and wrote down religiously where their moves should be. I soon found this stultifying. I began to ask myself how the barrier between what belongs to life – the chatting, the cups, the coats and bags – and work in the space could be broken down.

When I became a director I started by not having the room set up before the actors' arrival according to the usual layout, and got the actors into the space as soon as rehearsal began by simply asking for their co-operation in organizing the room. I dispensed with the directorial lecture, dispensed for the moment with the reading. I delayed the designer showing the model and the costume drawings until the second day. The actors criss-crossed the space, learned its contours, noticed the props and costumes lying around, moved chairs, adjusted a table, negotiated with each other. It created a far better atmosphere. The director can join in, become part of the workforce and at the same time see the actors from a distance as they move unselfconsciously, making the space their own.

The very first thing a director can do is suggest something as mundane and simple as finding and organizing a definite place for all the extraneous coats and bags and get stage managers to help move some tables to that area. This will become in time the centre of the actors' private off-stage area – if there is enough space around and behind it and a bit of stacked furniture, an old sofa and some leftover stuff from former rehearsals. The actors will soon hack out personal little nests.

Think carefully beforehand where this area should be since as actors arrive and leave, taking coats, forgetting scripts, they should not be in the eye-line of those rehearsing. I always get up and start to move my own coat there and I ask the stage managers to locate themselves and their tables somewhere else too – even if it is only a small move off-centre of the playing area. Suddenly everyone is on the move through the space.

This all may appear mundane and nothing at all to do with directing but it is about a skilful building of atmosphere. The atmosphere of the rehearsal room is of vital importance, no matter how well maintained or ramshackle it happens to be. The room must be clean. If there is no-one else whose job it is to do it, get there early and get a broom and a mop and do it yourself, if necessary. This shows a respect for the actor and his physical ease, especially when there are regular movement classes or physical improvisations. But at an altogether deeper level, at the level of the group as a well-functioning work group, all this organization and attention to detail and aesthetic gives the impression of control and boundaries, of a process at work where all are taking part. As you start to help organize the space, the actors sense there is someone who is both securely at the helm but also forms part of a joint enterprise.

During this first period of simple re-organization, I quite deliberately make a small gesture of physical contact with everyone in the room – a hand on the shoulder, a touch on the arm. This breaks through the unspoken barrier of untouchability with which we surround ourselves as we move through a culture of streets and trains and strangers. It enables the director to approach the actor – without being creepy or suggestive – on the level of the gesture as well as the word. A fingertip touch on the back, a breath out, can replace reams of explanation at a later stage of rehearsal.

So once the first introductions are over and the room organized, I try hard to keep everyone up on their feet – and I mean everyone – stage management, observers, assistants – anyone who cares to stay in the room – up into the space as quickly as possible and I would never dream in the first hours of seeming to ask them to do any acting.

Start by asking questions that draw on the ordinary biographical facts of people's lives. To get actors unselfconsciously into the space, I invoke an imaginary map traced out on the floor, and the group separates and go to the place on the map where they were born and then each in turn tells us, say, his full name, his birthplace and his birth date. It is amazing how much you can learn about the group. I return to anthropological days and sometimes think I should write a monograph on the different companies with whom I work.

Then you can ask other questions. The process can go many ways: where they first went to school, where their parents met, where they had their first kiss, where they did their first job. The actors move across the map, listen to each other's natal accents, tell stories about their grandmother or great aunt or where they did a hated apprenticeship in engineering or why they were born in a castle, and finally as the questions get nearer to the present day, they will invariably congregate around the very place in which you all now find yourselves. Now you can zoom in, change the imaginary map and let them imagine the whole room as a particular town, for instance. They can stand where they live, where their favourite restaurant is: make it up as you go along. The actors move across the map as each question is posed. There is a lot of scope for jokes and laughter – the unfortunate who never left Rotherham or Detroit until he was twenty, or the confession of a hated second name. Then you can begin to share anecdotes: how their parents met or how they came to work in the theatre. A strange kind of anthropological show starts. You all begin to get a sense of the myriad accidents of fate that have brought you together at this point in time for this group project. And so almost imperceptibly we begin to do what we are paid to do: tell stories and listen.

Reading the play

The first reading is sometimes regarded as the litmus test of whether the casting process has been successful, and actors are expected to pull out some kind of rough approximation of performance at this point to reassure everybody. In fact, I have known actors in American productions fired from the job after the first reading, so untrusting of the rehearsal process were the producers. Many modern actors are not accustomed to result-led work, and certainly English actors often do not present with results at the beginning of rehearsals. Many a fine actor only makes decisions slowly. They give very little indication at a formal seated read-through of the discoveries and wonderful inventiveness they will come up with later. Part of the joy of directing is the satisfaction of having created the atmosphere and understood the process by which the actor can present you with aspects of the play you would never have dreamt of beforehand.

I often put the first reading into the rehearsal space by having chairs set out in a rough crescent shape in the middle of the rehearsal room and getting the actors to move into the space for their scenes, choosing any chair they wish, and moving out of it again on their exits. This means the reading is less tense and more useful. By the day of the reading the actors are more relaxed and often begin to move around spontaneously and the play begins to assume some kind of volume in the space and everyone understands the to and fro of their characters. This way you perceive in space and time how the narrative unfolds. The work on the text then proceeds alongside concomitant work in the space: text work happens only in the space and never sitting around a table locked into talking about things rather than trying to embody them.

Listening and hearing

The audience hears only once a text the actors and director have read, discussed, pored over, and have heard or spoken perhaps hundreds of times. A basic part of the director's job is to make sure the audience hears. It is usually a relatively simple job to do. Once in the performance space, send some of the company to the back of the auditorium, leave some on the stage and get them to call and speak some of their lines to each other, gauging the pitch and volume required to reach each other. This is an area where a voice coach can do much work, but extending the voice to communicate with the room is usually a matter of the actors knowing the distance their voices must reach; the wish to communicate drives everything else – breath, pitch and volume. If an actor does not have the vocal equipment to project the voice to the far corners of the space, there is often nothing that can be done in the short time of a rehearsal period. This has to be a consideration at the casting stage.

Much more important though is to ensure the audience can listen, understand and respond. The text is of its nature concentrated, full of meaning, honed in its language and expression, its rhythms and buried turns, twists and manipulations. How can the director listen to the text at every hearing as if for the first time? This will be an act of concentration and an assumed amnesia. You must forget you know the text. Listen only to what the actors say. Put the script aside. Too many directors have their heads buried in the written word. It is not the written word that comes on the stage: it is the actors breathing, living, speaking. Reserve your attention, care and concentration for them. They are the bearers of the text; it can only live through them.

Young directors know they have to listen to the text but in the age of sound bites and short concentration spans catered for on film and television, their powers of listening have not been trained and extended. Often a young director has asked me forlornly, 'What am I listening for?'

You might answer 'the sense' until you are blue in the face. It is too generalized a response and often seems to defeat and depress a young director, although even experienced directors allow onto the stage actors who horribly mangle the sense of text.

Ponder for a moment what happens as a text hits your ears. Without at this point delving too much into psychological and physiological explanation, a director can make use of a relatively simple construct. Imagine the process – complex and super fast – that takes place in the brain as words hit the ear. Take a simple situation: a character looks at another and begins:

'I am going to ...'

Your ear takes in the sense that the character is about to do something and then your brain comes up with a question: what? Answer: do something or go somewhere. The brain then expects an answer to the puzzle this simple phrase has set. Say the phrase then continue with an answer: 'I am going to cry' or 'I am going to Birmingham.' The verb cry or the noun Birmingham are the satisfying conclusion to the question implied as you hear the first part of the line. Cry or Birmingham have to be spoken – and most of the time in normal human intercourse are spoken – to the listening ear in such a way as to satisfy it, to answer the question inspired by the first part of the phrase. But then say if we get:

'I am going to cry if ...'

Remember all this is happening in a fraction of a second in that most sophisticated computer which is the human brain: if ... what?

'I am going to cry if you don't ...'

If you don't what?

And so on: a text unravels in a complex split-second by split-second sequence of answers to millions of unconscious questions. So it is useful to imagine the audience in subconscious interrogative mode and to put yourself consciously into it as you listen carefully to actors speaking the text as they rehearse. Do the answers land upon the ear so that what is said is completely intelligible? You are asking silently all the time what, who, where, and why and by listening carefully you check that you are receiving the answers. So it is much more than hearing which you are practising; it is listening, and listening for easy sense. In working carefully at first rehearsals to make the text listenable, clear and unmannered, the director and actors are laying the groundwork from which any further work on actions, character, flow, rhythm and dynamic can then be built.

You cannot find the music of the text, or vibrate emotion through it or subtly fill it with breath and feeling or musicality without first finding the simplicity of its sense.

The capacity to listen for non-sense can be trained and honed. Good directors have what is called a marvellous ear. They have listened for sense and musicality all their lives. All directors should try from the very beginning of their training or experience to listen to the spoken word and ask themselves how it could be clearer and more beautiful to the ear.

Some actors, when asked to simply render the sense of the line, suppose clarity lies in clear enunciation of every word – a sort of spelling out of a sentence as if the hearer is deaf. This only gives rise to what I call typewriter speaking which bullies the ear. It is painful to listen to. Then there are those actors who try to explain the language as they speak it, over-colouring it, adding gesture and emotion as if the characters they are with on stage speak another language and need a physical and vocal show. They do not trust the simplicity of the words. They have no feel for the tune of sense making, which is as much about de-emphasis as emphasis. They feel they have to do something to the language to make it more intelligible. Usually they have to do less.

The director can listen for what kind of sentence they are trying to say, get them to put it into their own words, speak it to someone as they would in everyday life and then taking the sensation of it, speak again in the words from the text. This usually reminds them how sense is conveyed simply.

Actors are sometimes reluctant to do this very basic type of work on sense for fear of beginning to speak as if by rote, of losing their individuality. They feel they have to bring something individualistic to their speech. Here is an exercise that might re-assure them and you that you can never rob an actor of his personality by helping him to make sense.

Take this line of Robbie Burns' poetry: 'My love is like a red, red rose.' It is a statement. If you take a group of actors and decide together exactly how this sentence has to be spoken for its full sense to fall easily upon the ear, and they each in turn speak it, listen and even change their delivery until everyone utters the agreed sense of the line, you may imagine that each actor becomes indistinguishable from the other. This may in fact be the actor's private dread: they will lose any individuality. But you will all discover this does not happen at all because actors working to an agreed sense and emphasis utterly retain their personality, their particular timbre of voice, the quality of breath: their uniqueness. All they have in common is lucidity. This is the firm base from which all subsequent work on the text can then proceed.

'Listen for the sense,' I used to tell young directors and they would sit before the actors with sweaty palms, not really knowing what they were listening for. So at the risk of being simplistic here are a few basic tools the director can use to hone their listening skills.

One of the most basic tools in the director's kit is good old-fashioned grammar.[1] A fundamental knowledge of the following is useful:

- statements
- commands
- questions
- personal and possessive pronouns.

It is not enough of course to have a theoretical knowledge of them. A director should understand sensuously how each lands on the ear.

To this should be added:

- lists
- parentheses
- subordinate clauses.

Now every bit of text the actors speak can be listened to for these constructs. It is, though, of no possible use to the actor or the audience just to make a theoretical analysis. What the director must proceed to discover is a way to get the actor to deliver to the audience's ears and understanding, the kind of sense they are making. Go to your shelves, pick up any play and just take apart a speech. And listen for the following.

Statements

When the actor has a statement to speak it is important that they deliver the simple sense of it. If it is not clear, the actor has to be encouraged to 'go statement': as in 'the cat sat on the mat.' Who ... did what ... where?

The personal pronoun

I might subtitle this: the curse of the personal pronoun. Listen to the sense of this phrase if the personal pronoun is emphasized.

'My love is like a red, red rose.'

This suggests that there is another love in contention – that the speaker's love is like a rose and someone else's perhaps isn't. But the real force of this line lies in its emphasis on the quality of the beloved, not to whom he or she belongs. *My* love hints at the sense of my as opposed to some other love. Be vigilant about the over-emphasis of:

- my your his her our their
- mine yours his hers ours theirs
- me you him her us them
- I you he she we you they.

These are only rarely the important operative words in a text, and the over-emphasis of them is nearly always a symptom of an actor struggling with false energy to inject emphasis into a speech where it is not justified and obscures the sense. Again and again in rehearsal as I hear an actor emphasize 'I' and 'my', I use the same formula: 'We know it's you or yours, what else more important do we need to know?'

Questions

The question is the great litmus test of whether speech is proceeding truthfully, passing from character to character in reciprocal pressures. If a question is written but is not truly asked by the actor, how can the action truthfully proceed? A character on stage would in truth not answer a question that is not put, and yet if the text involves an answer, the actor replying has to proceed as if the question had been put. The text begins to sink into a quagmire of untruthfulness and the characters are soon no longer truly responding to what they have heard but what they have to imagine they have heard. They stop talking to each other and merely deliver their part of the text: their speech does not arise from what is actually happening in the present between them.

There is of course the rhetorical question which is asked to hammer home an argument and is not expecting an answer. If the question is rhetorical a response from the other character will not be written and this is in itself an emphasis of the force of pressure the speaker of the rhetorical question is exerting. Make sure you can hear questions really being asked.

Commands

If a command is given and, of course, the means an actor uses to convey a command can be manifold, moving by many degrees from coaxing to threatening, the reciprocating character is obliged to respond – to obey, to hesitate, to object, to defy. The command is a powerful tool of reciprocal pressuring and throws the audience's attention resolutely on the character pressured. What will be their response?

Lists

The list involves an accumulation of adjectives, of phrases, of arguments and has an inbuilt energy within it as it proceeds to muster thought upon thought, building an edifice of persuasion. The actor proceeds as it were from the bottom of a hill, phrase upon phrase, until he reaches a summit: the conclusion of the list. In complex speech, a list is often made up of subordinate clauses and within these clauses may be other grammatical features – rhetorical questions, thoughts in parentheses, other lists: all these have to be untangled and delivered with proper emphasis to reinforce the sense of the argument.

I use a very simple tool to help actors find the sensation of what happens as they assemble lists, which involves yet another return to a cooking analogy. I ask them to imagine a favourite recipe and then to improvise a scene where they are giving someone the shopping list of ingredients. They then take the sensation of that simple list – a buoyancy of thought, of breath, of upward intonation – into a text involving more complex constructs of description or argument. They have to be encouraged to think forwards and not to lose vocal energy and build until they reach the very end of the list.

Subordinate clauses

These are explanatory or qualifying remarks, adjuncts to the main statements. An actor's speech easily becomes unintelligible if equal emphasis is given to subordinate clauses as to the main arguments which they are being organized to strengthen. These thoughts (which can be marked lightly in pencil by brackets) are of their nature adjuncts to the main statements and are characteristic of rhetorical speech or speech that seeks to argue. They are the sign of a lively mind and a teeming brain: an articulate person. The sensation in the ear is that they float above and around the main thrust of the argument – usually a statement – and bring finally great emphasis to bear upon the resolution of the statement. To use another metaphor, they are tributary thoughts to the main river course of the argument that join it at its conclusion to make a pressure that can break down resistance.

On my desk on this spring morning lies a copy of *Richard III* and I have opened it randomly at Act V Scene 3: a speech of Richmond to his soldiers.

Read it and look for statements, questions, lists, subordinate clauses – and keep a wary eye on personal pronouns.

> More than I have said, loving countrymen,
> The leisure and enforcement of the time
> Forbids to dwell upon: yet remember this,
> God and our good cause fight upon our side;
> The prayers of holy saints and wronged souls,
> Like high-rear'd bulwarks, stand before our faces;
> Richard except, those whom we fight against
> Had rather have us win than him they follow:
> For what is he they follow? truly, gentlemen,
> A bloody tyrant and a homicide;
> One raised in blood, and one in blood establish'd;
> One that made means to come by what he hath,
> And slaughter'd those that were the means to help him;
> A base foul stone, made precious by the foil
> Of England's chair, where he is falsely set;
> One that hath ever been God's enemy:
> Then, if you fight against God's enemy,
> God will in justice ward you as his soldiers .... .

Where is the first statement?

'The leisure and enforcement of the time forbids me to dwell upon more than I have said.'

Where is the first command?

'Yet remember this,'

Where is the second statement?

'God and our good cause fight upon our side;'

Where is the third statement?

'The prayers of saints and wronged souls stand before our faces;'

First qualifying phrase

'like high-rear'd bulwarks,'

Where is the fourth statement?

'Those whom we fight against would rather have us win than him they follow:'

Second qualifying remark

'Richard except,'

First question

'For what is he they follow?'

An answer to the question in the form of three statements:

'A bloody tyrant and a homicide;'
'A base false stone,'
'One that hath ever been God's enemy;'

Now begins a long list involving the use of 'one':

'one raised in blood and one in blood established;'

Finally you are brought to a conclusion beginning with the word

'Then,'

The skill is not only to understand the ingredients of the speech but to listen carefully to the actors and to make sure they communicate these underlying structures to the audience. Only then can they proceed to colour, to invest, to characterize the speech. Get the actors to lay out vocally the ingredients of the speech first and all their subsequent acting choices will be thoroughly grounded in sense.

Props, clothes and furniture

I am fanatical about props. I hate to see an actor empty handed trying to mime a prop since through long experience I have learned that the physical sensation of an object in the hand can transform the imaginative process. An actor can find a character simply in the work involved in the manipulation of the right prop. Because I work in a relatively unplanned way within an early rehearsal, devising scenarios, switching between text and improvisation, continually looking again at sequences, I am constantly asking for unanticipated props: Is there a large sheet? Let's scatter some clothes beside the bed! Write a telegram! We need a parcel!

Having the right prop, even the right kind of substitute for a prop, can make the difference to whether an actor begins to break through in a scene or not. There is some sensual spark between the actor and the material in hand. Take this scenario, for instance. A letter is to be delivered to an apartment in Paris: an actor transforms himself into a messenger boy and stands knocking at a rehearsal room door in a peaked cap with a letter in his hand. The occupant of the apartment – a young wife   rises from her bed, comes to the door and takes it trembling, and despite her rising panic, finds the change for a tip and manages an exchange of civilities. The door closes. She hesitates, feels for a moment the smoothness of the envelope, and then tears it open and finds the words she has been dreading. 'We regret to inform you of the death of your husband …'.

Then we skip to the next day. A letter arrives in the same way – this time when she opens it, out falls her dead husband's Croix de Guerre. Who sent it? Why? How did they come by it?

These are the scenarios we devised to arrive at a speech in *Remembrance of Things Past* which Gilberte begins 'When Robert died, I received a letter …'. The letter does not appear in the play but by making the props and using them well in rehearsal, the actress was able to discover her grief and mystification at her husband's secret obsessions – for the Croix de Guerre has been dropped by him on the floor of a male brothel.

And if ever the text refers to someone's work, it is astonishing how an actor can become transformed if he learns precisely how to do it and gets the feel of the work process and the tools of his trade in his muscles. This goes for everything from the playing of a violin to assembling a Gatling gun. I might judge immediately how good the work is going to be on O'Casey's play *The Plough and the Stars* by how believably in the very first moments the actor playing Fluther sets about mending the lock of the door.

In an early rehearsal of *The Mother* by Brecht there was a scene in which a small revolutionary group printing leaflets is raided by the police. I did everything I could to encourage the assistant stage manager to find a rudimentary printing machine and in the end we found a simple manual mimeograph – not the right period but the best we could do. The actors, calling each other by their character names, in basic costumes pulled together from a hamper of old clothes, and in a simple room they devised for themselves from rehearsal furniture, worked out how to take this machine apart, hide the parts and put it together again. Then they did it again and again until they could do it at speed without anyone having to speak. It took half a day. All kinds of things began to happen – someone got a nickname, someone else kept dropping things, someone understood the best order in which to do things: they became a very believable group. When they next met to rehearse, and rather complacently started to rehearse the printing, I had carefully primed other members of the cast to stage a police raid ensuring the revolutionary group would have only just enough time to realize what was happening and to dismantle the machine and hide the parts. But it all needed great concentration. I had to watch the group at work on the printing and give correct signals to the police to start first to bang on the door and then to finally break in. In a sense, by my conscious timing of it, it was artificial but the reactions of the group hard at work and not suspecting anything but a re-run of the former rehearsal was going to take place, were only too real. One moment they were assembling and printing and the next, they had to go into survival mode. The work with this one essential prop gave the group its cohesion, hierarchy, courage, ingenuity and cunning – and incidentally solved in one fell swoop how the machine parts might be hidden. Of course, we developed the scene in detail over subsequent rehearsals, working into the text, and perfecting each gesture of their panicky behaviour in exact detail but the essential believability of the group coalesced because of work with this one prop.

The same principle applies to elements of clothing and to furniture. Get a very good substitute if not the actual object or garment into the rehearsal room straightaway. It will do most of the work for you. This is where a rail of costumes, and any miscellaneous props, accessories and pieces of material that might take the stage management's fancy, come in useful. The group can start to assemble their own costumes in scenarios, furnish rooms, construct carriages and circus rings, kitchens and battlefields. It was an actor and a designer playing around together with a shirt, crumpled newspaper and sticky tape who, in the opera Gawain, devised a head that could be cut off a torso which then mounted a horse and rode off.

Actable research

The actor is in the space telling stories. Now how can we enter the world of the play? Try to think of ways that research into the background of the play can lift off the page and into the space. Make it above all actable.

I try to organize before rehearsal as much visual research as possible: relevant books of photographs, or reproductions of paintings and I have to hand some music of the period the actors will research. Then I try to have a rail of costumes, some hats, piles of sheets, off-cuts of different materials, scissors, pins, sticky tape, rolls of paper, shoes, sticks, and miscellaneous props and accessories: anything that might be useful in constructing an image or making an idea materialize: a sort of grown-up version of a dressing-up or rainy-day box you make for a child.

The actors can then look through all the images in the books and research material, and choose one that interests them. Then they become the director for a moment. You can ask them to try to re-create the texture and shape of the image using other actors. They describe to them the shape of the clothes they want them to find, the details of the background, the mood of the image. It is often better for the participants not to be shown the actual image until they have tried to re-create it imaginatively by the 'director' evoking it through putting into words the feel of the image, the mood, the atmosphere, the shapes the figures make. This means the group sets about expressing the image through sensation, trying on different pieces of costume, making props from torn-up paper, hats from scarves and feathers. I always go in and help the actors – quickly making things with card and scissors or pinning an old costume at the back, and immerse myself in the easy creativity of the group. You finalize the image by pretending to take a snapshot of it. Then everyone can study the printed image and make suggestions as to how what has been made in the space can be changed or improved. Further adjustments can be made, relationships inferred, narratives implied.

This work with an image in the space can be infinitely developed. Try getting the actors to move across the space into the image, creating a pretend movie sequence. The group will start to work in an unselfconscious way, handling costumes and props, adjusting their positions, arranging furniture, inventing names, improvising lines. Get them though to be sparing with words – the calling of a name or phrase is usually sufficient – as we are here intent on sensation in the space, not improvising text.

For instance: take an early twentieth-century French photograph of a family and friends in the country on a picnic. Make a sequence that moves into and out of the image. See what happens if the youngest enters the space and looks around, calls out over a field that he has found the right picnic spot in the woods and everyone gathers there. They bustle in, a blanket is spread out, people sit down, a man leans against a tree on the periphery, lights a cigarette, the child throws a ball in his direction, a young woman gathers it up and joins the young man under the tree, the child tugs at her skirt but she hands him the ball and gestures him away, the child wanders back to the picnic, the couple are alone.

Enlarging upon a still image in this way, the actors, with the director's careful intervention, can move from snapshot to scenario hardly noticing that they are doing so. Something interesting starts to happen: the actors react to the shape and feel of the costume, they put themselves into the skin of those figures in the images they are shown. You can add music too. If someone plays the piano or a fragment of a song can be incorporated, you can play this as the scenario settles into stillness or as it starts. The permutations of this image work are endless.

When I started work on *Remembrance of Things Past*, I knew that one of the young actors in his first job and at his first professional rehearsal, played the piano. He found himself nervously improvising at the keyboard. As the images built there were calls: 'We need some Satie chords' and 'Do you know any rags?' In this way we created from flapping silk the waves lapping the shore at Balbec and the girls running and jumping them, tearing off their stockings and button boots. Another contrasting image was a Brassai photograph of a group of young women lying in a tousled heap on a divan in an opium den. Minus the opium, these were the images we used when the girls lay on the cliffs after running helter-skelter towards their picnic spot. Another Brassai image of two half-dressed young men in a night-club, one with a tie hanging down his naked back, their arms around each other's shoulders, found its way into the brothel scene which was created three weeks afterwards. The actors knew they had created these images from the first days of rehearsal. They discovered how they walked in the room, ran along the beach, how they danced to an old tune on a piano, how they breathed. They knew them in their bones. They owned the images.

Scenarios of events previous to the play

One of the most useful tools I've developed over time is a method of sifting the text for previous events referred to by the characters or implied by the text but which we don't actually see in the play. I then get the actors to recreate these episodes – swiftly, spontaneously, making impromptu props and costumes from whatever is lying around the room. The actors should abandon self-criticism and try to have fun. This often involves the whole company playing in myriad episodes alluded to in scenes in which their characters are not involved. They simply respond to what they hear in a phrase or line and become whatever character is needed in the moment. They all begin to discover what in Hollywood screenwriting manuals is called the 'back story': what has happened before a scene starts – sometimes far back in the past, sometimes in the immediate moments leading up to the opening line in a scene.

I call these scenarios rather than improvisations because although the actors work in their own words (or often with no words at all), or I give them simple lines to say, there is a definite narrative which they are trying to discover. Pure improvisation, on the other hand, is open-ended and completely unplanned. This work is much more controlled and with an aim in sight – a moment in the text.

Take the opening scene of Ibsen's *Hedda Gabler*, for instance. Tesman's aunt Julie arrives at her nephew's new house early one morning and the scene opens with the maid, Berthe, explaining that the couple are still asleep, having arrived late the night before with all their luggage, some of which Hedda had insisted on unpacking and which Berthe is still trying to organize. The scene opens with Berthe and Julie in the drawing room. Where exactly are they in the room? How is the furniture disposed? What props are around? At what precise moment of their morning's conversation do we, the audience, join them?

The first line of a scene is rarely the first line of a conversation. We more often than not catch the characters mid-flight. And yet much staging of first moments of scenes has no sense of movement in it. It is static and literally, blocked. Blocking[2] is a term I have never understood since the director's task would seem to be to unblock the actors, not the reverse.

A clue is there in the text when Berthe says there is nowhere in the room to put the flowers Aunt Julie has brought. This implies all the surfaces are already covered in the contents of trunks and suitcases and flowers. Aunt Julie decides she must not wake the couple and then we learn of their arrival at the port the previous evening, a hint at Hedda's reluctance to take Julie home in her carriage, and the presence there of Judge Brack. Taking phrases from the text, the director and actors can quickly invent a scenario with the bustle of the port, the porters and the luggage, the imperious Hedda, the fond welcoming aunt, Tesman torn between the two women, Brack's offer to take the aunt home in his carriage, his role as the purchaser of the house furnishings; then the arrival of Tesman and Hedda at the new house, the maid's nervousness, Hedda's demands, the departure for bed. In this way too, the actors discover the background to Julie's early morning visit and finally how exactly she has arrived in the drawing room from the outer door, and the stage picture in which the first line of text would most naturally appear.

Within only a short opening scene, scenarios of Hedda's imperiousness; of Berthe's past service with the family; of the aunt's financial investment in the new house; of Brack's manipulation of the expenditure; of the dependence of Julie's sick sister; of Tesman's cosseted youth and the full emotional import of Julie's new hat which Hedda is shortly going to deride. All this can be explored in short improvised sequences where the actors and the rest of the company paint vivid pictures and more importantly experience sensuously the full import of what short references in the text allude to.

What the director does is improvise in their way too: setting up the scenario in as specific a way as possible, going back over them with changes if they do not quite arrive at what the text precisely suggests, suggesting lines or activity or attitude, but looking always to the text for guidance. Some scenarios can last for moments – Julie and the child Tesman at his father Joachim's deathbed. Some may last for a few minutes – Julie trying to choose the right hat. They all add a texture, complexity and depth to the playing of the surface text. They can also provide absolutely truthful stage pictures bearing no resemblance to what empty theoretical blocking would arrive at.

More importantly still, it gives the actors a sensuous hold on the text, a sense that they have really experienced what they refer to. The text is spoken in a quite new way once these scenarios have been discovered.

The play as an abnormal event

The dramatic event arises when what is usual is disrupted. Early scenarios of the uneventful, usual day in the world of the play – of the day without the celebration of a nameday on a Russian estate or a day without the arrival home of a mother from Paris or how life was for Tesman with his doting aunt when he had not yet married Hedda Gabler – looked at carefully by the director and sifted for a significant image, or developed and simplified, underscored with music or heightened into even a single physical gesture stretched out of naturalism: all this can feed into the production, giving you a movement language to call on later in the work. Once you have the ordinary life of the characters, you can explore the changes that the dramatic event and unexpected catastrophe impose upon them, how their physical responses change under the force of circumstance.

In Lorca's play *The House of Bernada Alba*, I knew there had to be a profound physical transformation in my English actresses if they were to embody their Andalucian characters. With a Spanish movement director, Isobel Baquero who had studied both flamenco in Spain and movement for actors with Jane Gibson in London, we got the daughters to each make a room of their own anywhere in the rehearsal space and to start to move through a typical day from six in the morning until eleven at night, creating images as the stage manager rang out the hours by striking a bell at five-minute intervals. They all found striking personal images for each of the hours. As they began to work in detail on the text, we added all kinds of detail to the movement work: the dance of the Sevilla, dexterity with the shawl and the fan, nimble telling of their rosaries, their demeanour in mass, eating lunch on the patio, secretly peering through the grilles of windows, the breathless heat of mid-afternoon, the restlessness of the siesta hours, their need for fresh air, the impulse to dance, their frustrated sexual yearning – a mass of physical details and images was accumulated. Then we devised scenarios which had some bearing on events in the text – where ordinary life changed when they were forced into mourning – where the girls would hide a photograph or sentimental keepsake, how they would react if they were telling jokes and their mother entered the room, how they would organize the sewing of a trousseau, the effect of hearing men's voices singing in the fields.

This, first done mainly in movement with just a name or phrase spoken to help the action, developed then alongside detailed examination and speaking of the text – doing it, not talking about doing it. The text then became embedded in a groundwork of sensuously discovered gesture and movement.

The work on the everyday world of the play takes time and enormous concentration and you have to be brave enough to decide what to keep, what to discard, when to move on and how you might develop the fragile beginnings of gesture, image and movement. In the end, this part of the work which comes unforced from the actor improvising in the space is the crucible from which original and authentic physical expression is made. The good director discovers early that the actors' imaginations harnessed to that of the designer and the director will bring results far more than the sum of the parts. What happens in the room is better than what happens in one person's imagination. After all the people in the room exist, your fantasy does not. We have to be concerned with what the audience can experience, what the actors can embody, not what the director might have imagined. The director's task must be to find simple easy ways to release the actors, coax their impulses into physical expression and to sift the results for what is useful, useable and understandable by the onlooker.

9

FORGING A DIRECTING LANGUAGE

One day in a workshop, I asked actors what were some of the more terrible notes directors had given them:

'Could you be more universal?'
'Well, she's just a bitch, isn't she?'
'Be more Russian.'

They laughed. Otherwise, they would have wept.

Every director has to find a way to communicate with the actor. You will slowly forge your own language and every time you begin a new project with a new set of actors and another play, the language you use will subtly have to change. But it is worth looking at the basic lineaments of acting, to remind yourself of what you are looking for and why, and most importantly how to help, not hinder, the actor. The least you can do is not to stop actors dead in their tracks. Why is the actor so vulnerable? It is because the sensations they rely on to lead them to a character are often at the beginning elusive and barely graspable. It is as if the actor is moving in the dark, half-paralysed, groping for something. Sometimes I can barely recognize some actors whom I have seen in wonderful, inventive and energetic performance when they are still at the stage of creeping about the rehearsal room trying to get to grips with things – a walk, a gesture, a timbre of voice. They are a shadow of their stage selves.

In these first stumbling beginnings – and beginnings can last for a long time – the actor often does not really know what he is after. The sensation is buried somewhere in his body and subconscious and is only barely flickering with life. Forcing the pace at this point, showing a lack of understanding of this delicate process, giving a crass note about externals, does not just delay the actor, it actually kills the burgeoning sensation stone dead. The actor simply cannot get back to it. It eludes him for good. It is as if a premature baby has been smothered with one swift press of a pillow.

Therein lies the actor's vulnerability. And that is why actors sense very quickly whether a director is in tune with their needs and is going to help them develop a performance. It is not over-sensitive on the actors' part. It is not narcissism. It is practical, self-evident, empirical. This is how acting works. The director has to stand the heat or get out of the kitchen.

Remember too there are languages apart from the spoken word. There is touch – to the actor's spine, to the diaphragm, to the breastbone. There is your breath, a sigh, a groan. You can make gestures of grasping, floating, building, lightening, pushing. You can clench your fist as the actor comes to a potent line, you can stretch out your arms as an actress runs to a child. The brilliant English director, Peter Gill, has a vast vocabulary of gestures – one (much fondly mimicked) as if he is shaking a heavy frying pan in each hand – and as he makes it, his words invariably taper away. But he really understands acting and his actors get a sense of what to try next which goes beyond what words could have expressed. Actors can respond to much more than language. You can go into the space and stand beside the actor and try to get a sensation of what they are striving for. Sometimes I can walk miles each day in a rehearsal room mingling constantly with the actors, looking at the set and the other characters from their point of view. Sometimes I go into the space to initiate a gesture or embrace with another character to give tacit permission for the actors to work in that way: to disinhibit them. At other times, I might remain immobile in my seat.

Here are some definitions often used in analysing the acting process that all directors should ponder and understand. I will call them by their common names, but each director must find his own simple vocabulary for talking to all kinds of actors about the basic processes of acting. Look at actors at work on stage, in films, on television. All the time, think what words could I have used to get the actor to find that? If I had been acting, what could have helped me?

Action

Acting is achieved not by thinking or talking or planning but by doing things. The most basic building block is what has come to be referred to as the action and this involves understanding what a character is trying to do to someone else. Beware though. Some actors, untrained or from another discipline or a different kind of training, will not necessarily understand this word. But descriptive word aside, it is important for any director to grasp the concept of this smallest building block in the actor's construction of a role. Action is what a character is trying to do to another character through each particular section of the text – a word, a line or a group of lines. Action is best expressed by a simple active verb:

- girl pleads
- mother denies
- girl demands
- mother threatens.

It is best understood in terms of reciprocal pressures. A girl exerts a pressure. A mother receives this pressure and exerts a pressure in response. The girl then tries another pressure (you can think of it also as a ploy or a forcing) and so the dramatic to and fro proceeds. And thus the situation changes, develops and comes to crisis with characters controlling and being controlled in turn, developing new traits under the pressure of new situations.

Means

Means is the term used to describe how the actor exerts the pressure: the means he uses. These are expressed as different emotional ploys, methods or processes. In pleading, actors can weep, have hysterics, abase themselves. They can whimper, they can appear helpless, winsome, charming, set out the facts rationally, succumb to despair, to breathlessness, to whining.

There are many ways to exert a pressure and the actor is in search of all the means at his disposal so that he can lay out in rehearsal a palette of possibilities. The proof of the pudding will be in the eating, because as each possibility is tried it will elicit a reaction from the other actors as well as a reverberation in the agent of it, and a sense of truthfulness for the director. It will perfectly accord with the intention in the text. It will feel right.

Directors have to be open, aware and sympathetically critical of all the choices they are shown and rely on their intuition and personal experience as to what works most truthfully in the situation: what releases the drama of the confrontation, what makes the scene flow, what makes the actors flow, what gives us an authentic glimpse of character. These actions or coercive pressures, built moment to moment, pressure to pressure, and often painstakingly worked through, coalesce into the stuff of drama.

Activity

Activity refers to a movement or gesture an actor makes. It should crucially not be confused with action. Activity is something the actor does physically – sits in a chair, stands at a table, looks in a mirror, pours a drink. An activity is something that emerges from the action. Gesture and the handling of props is part of the physical extension of action. The actor usually discovers activity or gesture from the inside out. A skilled director can encourage the further development of movement or gesture, can adapt its rhythm and suggest its repetition but it is best first spontaneously expressed in the working of the actions – then it has a completely organic and natural atmosphere about it, unforced and redolent with meaning.

Actors need to discover an activity, not be told to do one. So be careful about suggesting activity – often the resort of the inexperienced or insensitive director – when what the actor needs to find is the action. It is only once he knows the why that the actor begins to discover the how. To suggest an external activity – why not sit on the chair? pick the cup up from the table? – when the actor is struggling to find out something much more basic and essential to the playing of the scene, is irrelevant and distracting.

State

A state is what a character is in, not what they do.

State is evidenced in body language, the spine, the chest, the functioning of the breath, the nervous system, sweat, tears.

The actor can be in a state of excitement, fury, grief. But actors run into a brick wall if they try to play state and not allow their actions to be uppermost. Inevitably, a set of generalized physical and vocal characteristics will infuse the whole acting sequence like a colourwash and render a scene oddly undynamic, on one emotional note, the exchanges repetitive, untrue.

It is a difficult notion to understand theoretically, and that is why directors should always have some experience of the acting process. The actor finds he undergoes a changed physical state which corresponds with emotional changes: he can be out of breath, sweating, deathly calm, frantic, tense, ready to snap, on the verge of collapse. It is like, for example, having a temperature. If you have a high temperature, you are perhaps in a fever –restless, hot, sweating, breathless but within that physical state you still exert pressures – you are demanding, you cry out in pain for pity, beg a child to not forget you, give orders for what must be done in your absence or lie in silence bearing the pain, trying not to frighten a loved one.

The state is a given. On top of that, despite that, there are actions to play. A grieving man can be vengeful, angry, hysterically amused, sexual, contrite, hopeful, relieved – depending what his actions are. Look at any documentary interview with people at the extreme of experience and you will understand this vital difference between state, action and activity. Good directors have to have their antennae tuned for generalized or clichéd responses and to encourage the actor to find something more personal and particular. It will be there in a good text waiting to be dug out. Neither does character fully announce itself at the beginning of a play – any more than you see a whole personality at a first meeting. Character emerges gradually, exposed action by action and undergoing change under the pressure of events or other characters' reactions or plight. This change in character in reaction to events – evidenced, I always think, by that small phrase: 'courage is grace under pressure' – is the stuff of drama and especially of classic tragedy, when we see what started in promise and potential end in waste and pity.

Resistance

Resistance is a profound and complex part of acting and describes a character's capacity to push down or cover a strong feeling with the patina of another: to resist showing a strong inner emotion by laying another order of behaviour over the top: to be angry but to attempt to speak calmly, controlling the adrenalin of fury pulsing through the body, to suppress tears and force oneself to joke and laugh, to find something almost irresistibly funny but to manage to maintain a solemn demeanour. The sensation of this in the actor's body is one of inner turbulence being pressed down, like the effort of keeping an untroubled composure whilst feeling agonizing pain. A sort of physical and mental dialogue goes on within the body between the two imperatives and one just about wins. One way of exploring this is to suggest the actor firstly plays full out the emotion that is going to be resisted, then, keeping the heartbeat, adrenalin and physical tension pounding through the body, to press over the top of it an apparent calm or whatever surface behaviour the actor wants or needs to impose.

The understanding of this propensity to cover, to not be able to sustain cover and then manage to cover once again owes much to a psychological understanding of the complexity of the human mind and spirit. The person who is boastful and assertive may in reality use these characteristics to cover anxiety and insecurity: the sycophantic servant, class hatred and contempt; the attentive and affectionate husband, sexual insecurity, jealousy and control. This is where an interest in and understanding of psychoanalysis can be of great use to a director.

Cliché

A good director has to have her antennae tuned for generalized or clichéd responses and to encourage the actor to find something more personal and particular. I am always on the look-out for a knee-jerk reaction to character that simply relies on cliché rather than on truthfulness, on a received idea rather than on experience or observation.

One day in a workshop, the word 'wife' set off a clichéd reaction in an actress. In Shakespeare's play *Julius Caesar*, Julia, Brutus's wife, comes into a garden in the middle of the night to confront him. The actress felt she had first and foremost to be a 'wife' and all her decisions – her voice, her movement – were coloured by a sickly patina of what I can only describe as 'pained-loving' acting. A wife might love a husband (and often sadly she might not) but that does not alter her actions when she has woken alone in their bed and heard in the garden her husband talking conspiratorially to a group of unknown men. What is he doing awake in the middle of the night, not confiding in her or sleeping with her? Why has he been so pre-occupied of late, so rude and dismissive? The actress should consider how she might speak in the darkness, knowing that servants might hear her from the house, since surely she suspects what her husband is doing must be kept secret. What pressures might she then exert to get him to confide in her? This is a Roman woman who values her lineage, esteems her honour and has slashed her thigh to convince him that she is nobly able to withstand pain and is worthy of knowing his secrets. The notion of 'wife' needs to be re-thought according to specific circumstances and in individual terms. The scene has nothing to do with a sentimental twentieth-century notion of conjugal love such as you might see in a soap opera.

Acting abounds with these clichés, especially where women are concerned. Compare the kind of nonsense you see in the portrayal of prostitutes – sitting astride chairs and sporting tatty feather boas, walking with a wiggle in their hips – and what the experience might actually be, what the century, what the economic reasons, what the skill might be. Aching feet, boredom, children to bring up on your own, premature death from tuberculosis, a drug habit, a reassuring manner, easy charm, a strong wrist, a willing mouth and the skill to get it over and done with quickly. These truths have nothing to do with cliché.

Women are often expected to accept a completely clichéd view of their responses, especially their sexual ones. I remember my wry disbelief once when, at the performance of a Restoration comedy in Stratford-upon-Avon, a woman character emerged from a short sexual encounter behind a screen and we were encouraged to believe she had enjoyed it immeasurably because she was in too much pain to sit down. We were expected to believe in her ecstatic discomfort. Was the director from another planet? Yes, from planet cliché. Male cliché at that. But clichés abound in all areas of acting: the kind doctor, the brave soldier, the cunning criminal, the gibbering insane, the languishing lover, the man supposedly tip-toeing, the girl supposedly running, the lesbian, the cop. There are stock clichés to be found on every kind of stage which have nothing to do with truthful observation. You can always have a good laugh with a group of actors by getting them to perform a series of instant clichéd characters and see them for what they are – risible.

Recovery

Recovery is the experience a character has to go through vocally, physically and emotionally after the expression of intense feeling, experience or realization before he can continue to move, regain his breath, speak. You cannot throw a punch and immediately throw another without a movement to regain your balance and breath. If an actor is fully in touch with what he is experiencing and what pressure he is exerting on another and by what means he is doing it, there will be a flow of recoveries going on in any section of the dramatic unfolding of the story, all of them of different duration – chronos – and nature depending on the intensity of what is being played. Look for instance at someone actually crying and observe by what stages they recover their equilibrium: too often we are forced to try to believe a character who is sobbing one moment can simply launch full breath into a speech the next. This is because the actor has not either fully experienced the sensation of what caused them to sob – and much of crying is the effort not to – or the exertions of the actual sobbing itself and they have not allowed time for the character to go through the complex process of recovery: first to choose and then to manage, a change from one action into another. We could say that sobbing has not cost the actor anything.

All character decisions to change tack and direction of pressuring have an inbuilt truthful time to them, an experienced time. Actors often seem impelled to wade on through the words because they are there on the page, and do not explore the recovery from one physical or emotional sensation into another – and only then to let the words drop into their minds. This often leads to generalized acting. The actor has to discover the distinct separate thoughts that make up a change of tactic which are like tiny separate beats of music. For example: a character is leaving, he hears a sound, he stops, he listens, he realizes, he absorbs a shocking truth, he regains emotional equilibrium, he decides, he hesitates, he summons up courage, he turns, he goes towards the sound to confront the situation. Twelve separate beats in a seemingly simple moment. The clue will often be found in the turns and twists of the text as the character employs new means or actions to get what he wants and what each new thought and emotion costs him physically. But sometimes the beats occur in a moment of silence – they are there nevertheless. I believe the measure of a great actor often lies not just in what he does and says but in how he recovers and how minutely he is able to work through the beats of thought and impulse in a silence.

Intensity

The intensity a character brings to a scene is evidenced by the level of his physical state, how highly wound up or adrenalized he is, what the rate of heartbeat and breathing is, how much he is sweating or feeling nauseous; how much is at stake; what level his physical and emotional investment in an outcome is. Much of this can be investigated by looking at the previous experience the character has undergone before entering into the scene. This sensation cannot be arrived at through decision or thought, although actor and director have to study the text for clues and use their imagination and ingenuity, but is best achieved through physical action – running, jumping, getting the heart rate up or whatever may be required. Look at what the difference is between an actor running three steps from the wings to announce a terrible danger and one who has taken the trouble to enact seeing the danger, panicking about what to do and then running a hundred yards or so before entering the scene. If an actor is encouraged to find the right level of intensity, the director has suddenly marvellous detailed material to work from. Sometimes, when all else seems right – the actors are playing their actions truthfully, the text is clear, the story revealed – the scene still does not seem to work. This is the time to look again at intensity.

In the scene in Webster's *The Duchess of Malfi* where the Duchess with her children flees to Ancona and takes leave of Antonio, her secret husband, with danger pressing in from all sides, the scene simply did not work. Then my movement director, Liana Nyquist, suggested the actress Lola Peploe should be out of breath and pouring with sweat. She gave her a handkerchief and suggested she might use it to soak up the sweat on her breast and neck and to wring it with anguish. In Laban terms the character's psychological state would be expressed in wringing. This was working from the outside in. The actress thought for a moment how she could arrive at this more intense physical and emotional state. And so she wisely started the scene again, and trying to get the sensation more on the inside, ran out of the rehearsal room and down and up three flights of stairs dragging her maid, luggage and a perambulator with her. Although the scene needed two more weeks' rehearsal, she unlocked her physical and emotional intensity in it. From then on she kept the handkerchief in her pocket as a reminder that she might at any moment need to use it.

There is much to be learned by really studying how human beings actually react to agonizing circumstances, to the recall of grief or the recounting of extreme experience. For instance, you might do well to watch an excerpt from the great documentary *Shoah* by Claude Lanzman, where Abraham Bomba, a Holocaust survivor, while cutting a customer's hair in a barber's shop in present day Tel Aviv, recounts his war-time experience in the death camp at Treblinka in Poland, where along with about fifteen other barbers he was forced to cut off the hair of women prisoners before they were gassed.

You will see here:

- actions – to make us imagine the unimaginable, to convince, to plead for the camera to be turned off, to sear the picture on our minds ;
- activity – the meticulous attention to hair cutting, the snap of the scissors, the smoothing of the customer's hair, the wiping of sweat on his own face with a towel;
- resistance – pushing down feelings of distress; he has to take time – chronos – as he fights within himself to achieve his action: to do what he has undertaken: to bear witness; to make us believe what happened;

- recovery – the means he has to employ to regain equilibrium when he gets to the words 'wife' and 'sister' and before 'in the last moments of their life';
- state – highly nervous despite his efforts to resist, he is sweating, his voice is harsh as he strives to keep to the facts.

His intensity is high. So is his resistance. This makes for a terrible complexity. A recourse to easy tears or clichéd response on an actor's part is an insult to real human experience.

Directors can scour the fabulous resources of the internet for research. There again you can simply keep your eyes and your ears open. The world, your world, teems with people at the extremes of experience, good or bad: love, hate, violence, agony, joy, laughter – be it in New Orleans, Gaza or on the upper deck of a 29 bus.

Look out also for other factors that may affect the acting process, as follows.

Environment

Sometimes the actors need to mark a complete change of locality and atmosphere and this is nowhere more evident than when the action on stage moves from the inside to outside. Stepping outside affects the whole body language, the trajectory of the voice, the direction of the eyes and the release of the breath. There is a simple way to experience this: take the actors outside. In *Remembrance of Things Past*, there was a scene of a group of girls at a picnic on the cliffs at Balbec. Once we had explored the outline of the scene in the rehearsal room, I suggested the girls quickly gather some rehearsal props together, run outside the theatre and down to the banks of the Thames and set up their picnic there. They took a blanket, picnic baskets and a bicycle with them, running and chattering all the way. By luck the tide was out, it was a brilliantly sunny day and there were seagulls whirling overhead. Beside the river, they played the scene in their own words and then without losing concentration or energy, they ran back to the rehearsal room and tried to retain all that they had discovered outside. The essential intensity of energy was there – they were like a great breath of fresh air, full of youth, sun and high spirits. All they needed now was six weeks rehearsal to get back with the text to what they had discovered in five minutes improvisation.

Another enormous release for actors comes if a scene meant to be played in darkness is discovered in darkness. Again everything alters in darkness – the way the voice is pitched, the reliance on sensation all down the back of the spine, the heightened sense of danger. The director can alternate between rehearsing in the light and in the dark until the actors have darkness in their breath and under their skin. Once I found one of my most brilliant students, the Icelandic director Jon Gunnard, rehearsing a scene from *Macbeth* in the lavatory – the only place where he could plunge the actors into darkness.

What I am talking about here is essentially a release of energy: neither a forcing nor a blocking of it. When you have actually run up and down several flights of stairs and come into a scene, when you are actually in a darkened room, you are in a state of having to let something happen. You cannot control either your breath or your adrenalin and they dictate your rate of thought, action and speech. The actor is not so much working as letting go, letting things happen at the rate they can, not at the rate he might have decided on. This sensation is related to that moment of suspension in the swing when the actor does pure movement. You cannot dictate that either. This is where at a profound level, movement work and acting coalesce.

Energy

The word energy comes from the Greek and has within it the notion of no work in the sense that something is full of power and is not having to engender it. Energy was first envisaged as a stream of particles flowing. Thus a proper energy for actors is one without effort. They do not have to strain for it, but simply allow it to happen. I say 'simply', but true energy often arrives as a result of hours of rehearsal and is difficult to achieve. I suppose this is what is meant by flow, unimpeded sensation so that gesture, activity, emotion seem inevitable, unforced and effortless.

A good distinction to keep clearly in mind is the difference between the actor's energy and the character's. These are often confused and what you see is the actor's effort and not the level of intensity the character may need to be at. A reminder to let go of the acting effort and find the character's effort can make a great improvement in an actor's work.

Once when I was directing Yvonne Bryceland in *The Mother*, she was struggling to learn the Eisler song 'On Communism'. 'It's no good', she said, 'I can't sing it and I've tried and tried.' 'But Yvonne', I replied, 'you're not singing it. Your character is. The mother can sing it because it is something everyone around her must understand. She has to sing it because it is too important just to be spoken. She has to sing it despite its difficulty.' She then stood up and sang it.

Knowing the narrative

Keep your eyes and ears alert to the character's as opposed to the actor's knowledge of the narrative. Life is lived forwards. The character does not know what is going to happen. The actor knows. He has read the play. None of us, thank God, has read the script of our lives. We rarely know what we are going to say or do as daily events unfold. How carefree we were, we remember, before we heard the bad news. For the purposes of acting, it is vital that the actor never lets knowledge of the plot affect his playing of a particular scene: he does not yet know that his lover is lying, that he is saying goodbye to his mother for the last time, or that deliverance is near. Never allow the actor's knowledge to colour the character's. Make sure the actor is not playing knowledge of the end of the scene at the beginning of the scene.

Defending your character

The same has to be said for the actor's conventional moral judgement. It is important that a moral judgement of a character – that she is unliberated, that he is sexist, that he is racist, that she is petty – is not brought to bear on acting choices. For the purposes of truly discovering character, the actor must defend his character body and soul. He will play a scene well if he has discovered why a character lies, betrays or weakens: and it will always be for a perfectly good reason from the character's point of view. Indeed the character may feel his very survival depends upon it. The character feels justified: it is up to the audience to make judgements: it is up to the actor to defend his character.

A director should be able to perceive and to thoroughly understand these aspects of the acting process and to carefully suggest the precise areas where an actor might try to make changes.

When finding your own particular directing language, look to the tone of how you say things as well as the actual vocabulary. The tone should be emollient not dogmatic. Do not instruct but elicit. Do not tell, allow. Do not dictate, discover. I always ask a young director to abandon the word 'no' in the rehearsal room. Remember the actor may still be searching for something at the moment inexpressible and it is important not to stifle possibility. A language which suggests possible alternatives, full of 'what ifs', is what you should search for. Directors perforce have questions to put, but they should search always for what is sensuous, actable, a word or phrase that can set the imagination going. They can refer to behaviour they have read about, witnessed or experienced. They can refer to the subtleties of human psychology, defence mechanisms, projections, hidden fears, concealed feelings. They can and must return the actor to an examination of what his reactions would be in a particular circumstance and then to find how they can best mediate these feelings through the prism of that particular character. The actor answers best though by trying something – by acting.

If a scene is not working, look for:

- Lucidity of the text: is it clear?
- As actors speak the text ask the questions: What? Where? Who? – and ask out loud if necessary.
- Are the actors allowing what is said to them to affect them? Are they allowing the other character's lines to land on them?
- What is the action or actions? Are they right? How could they be altered?
- What means are the actors using? Should they be different?
- What changes in the physical disposition of characters in the scene when a new action is tried? Does this need more time? Does it need adjusting?
- How does a new physical arrangement reverberate through the characters?
- How much resistance to revealing an emotional state does a character have?
- Is an actor mistakenly playing state rather than finding it and then playing an action?
- What is the character's level of physical intensity? Should it be higher or lower?
- What is the previous experience to the scene on stage? Is the actor bringing on that exact previous experience? Is the previous experience accurate?
- Has the actor experienced what lies below a textual reference by improvising a scenario? Is the scenario exactly what the text suggests? Should you try a revised scenario?
- Is the actor playing actor's energy not the character's?
- Have characters read the script? Are they mistakenly assuming a knowledge they cannot yet have?
- Are the actors allowing recovery to take place?
- Does a new thought precede a new utterance?
- Is there at work a clichéd response to character or text?

Plate 1   Jack Murphy exploring period deportment with the cast of *Remembrance of Things Past*, National Theatre, 2002 (photo Catherine Ashmore)

Plate 2 Movement work informs every character. Final moment of *Remembrance of Things Past*, National Theatre, 2002 (photo Catherine Ashmore)

Plate 3 The little band of girls: image created from a Brassaï photograph of
opium smokers. Left to right: Anita McCann, Indira Varma, Marina Morgan.
Remembrance of Things Past, National Theatre, 2002
(photo Catherine Ashmore)

Plate 4 Image from the epilogue to *Fears and Miseries of the Third Reich*: a modern parallel of an earlier Brecht scene. Left to right: Rhik Samadder, Daniel Winder. Cochrane Theatre, 2007 (photo Alan Pitchforth)

Plate 5 Simple gestures stretched into heightened image. Left to right: Shona Morris, Yvonne Bryceland, Jenny Galloway, Patricia Franklin, Geoffrey Freshwater. *The Mother*, National Theatre, 1986 (photo Michael Mayhew)

Plate 6 Keeping calm and carrying on. Left to right: Di Trevis, Kevin Cahill, Stephen Warbeck in technical rehearsal of *The Mother*, National Theatre, 1986 (photo Michael Mayhew)

Plate 7 Mark Marlowe and Ruta Gedmintas in *The Duchess of Malfi*, Cochrane Theatre, 2006 (photo Alan Pitchforth)

Plate 8 The Jerwood Workshop, 2009. Left to right: Katherine Newman, Di Trevis, Beatriz Romilly (photo Matthew Wandless)

Plate 9 Sian Thomas and Alfred Molina in *The Taming of the Shrew*, Royal Shakespeare Company, 1984 (photo Donald Cooper)

Plate 10 Sian Thomas as a travelling player in the opening image of *The Taming of the Shrew*, Royal Shakespeare Company, 1984. The banner on the cart reads 'A Kind of History' (photo Donald Cooper)

Plate 11   The Revenger's Tragedy, Swan Theatre, 1987. Left to right: David Howey, Antony Sher, Jeremy Gilley, Henrietta Bess, Julie Legrand, Jim Hooper, Mike Dowling, Nicholas Farrell (photo Joe Cocks Studio Collection @ Shakespeare Birthplace Trust)

Plate 12 The masked pavane in *The Revenger's Tragedy*, Swan Theatre, 1987 (photo Joe Cocks Studio Collection @ Shakespeare Birthplace Trust)

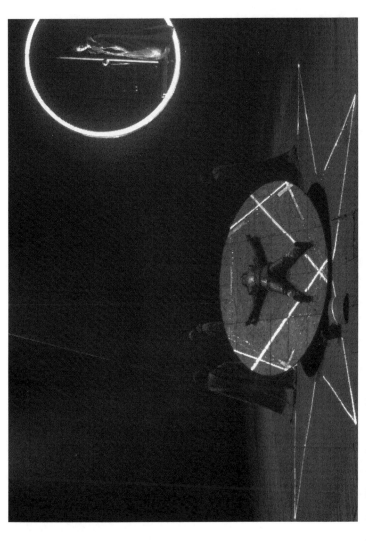

Plate 13 Circular disc etched in silver to outline a pentangle. Left to right: François Le Roux, Marie Angel. *Gawain*, Royal Opera House, 1991 (Image@Arenapal)

10

FLUID STAGING

I have already referred to fluid staging in my earlier chapter on Space. But it is at this stage in rehearsal that you can try to take some of the theory into practice. Of course, in pondering how we can get characters and objects into the space ahead of time and avoid laborious scene changes by stage hands in semi-darkness, we are not only playing with the space, we are also manipulating time and it needs a shift in your thinking about the disposition of the actor, the scenes and the way you rehearse to really keep a production flowing forward.

Take any play, somehow the more complicated the better – in this case I took the great Jacobean tragedy *The Duchess of Malfi* – and look at the scenes the play is divided into and further dissect it into rehearsable sections. A new section will probably occur when a new character enters. Look carefully at your sections and look to the future ones – one, two or three sections ahead. As you dispose your actors for the present section, think to the next: Who will it involve? What props might be needed? Where might they need to come from to aid the story-telling? Could a set of characters have entered earlier and be already in the space – not part of the immediate action, but waiting? As one set of characters moves forward for the next section, could another set for a later scene be brought on?

Most importantly, refuse to be dogged by literal or naturalistic considerations. Do not seek to explain figures in the space but experiment with the configurations of how they might be disposed and what enables the eye to accept a figure in the space but not dwell on it. Place an actor at the back of the space and have a scene played anywhere in front of him. If his eyes are not visible our eyes will not rest on him. Get the actor to stand in profile, eyes down. He may stay still or move in a slightly slower rhythm than normal. Experiment with this and you will soon see what attracts attention to the detriment of the scene being played and what does not.

A change of characters – a fluid movement on the stage – one lot flowing in to take over the audience's attention from the exiting characters, may also involve the movement forward of actors, objects and props for a much later scene. Characters for section 7 may well be brought into the space at the onset of section 3, together with a chair that will only come into its own at section 6 and does not necessarily have to leave the stage until section 9. It can get very complex. But you have to keep your wits about you and bring the actors into the thrill of the game too so that they can anticipate their entrances into scenes and find their way into the landscape of the stage area.

You cannot call the actors for rehearsal in the same way – actors are needed well before they actually play their scene; characters who would usually exit the space altogether might well assume positions somewhere on the stage so that they will be 'found' later. Lucky accidents occur – you suddenly see how a prop can be used or a figure in the space moved and new images open up. Sometimes a prop that was used in one scene can be transformed for use in another.

In a production of *As You Like It*, when Rosalind and her party decamped to the forest of Arden, they were laden with suitcases and luggage. When they exited the scene, I saw that if they left their luggage in front of two 'waiting' characters upstage, the suitcases became, with a light change and 'snow' falling, part of the Duke's forest encampment, then later trestles for an improvised table under the trees and finally piled on a wagon, the support for Adam as he was carried off exhausted, night falling, by the foresters.

For a long time I thought about what language the theatre could use to indicate the passage of time. And what was there in the theatre that could aid me in flowing scenes together swiftly and effortlessly without the predictable punctuation of darkness and scene changes. We all know the Hollywood device of a shot of a clock with the hands speeded up, of the leaves of a calendar flying away in the wind. Time, it tells us, has passed. I found my answer in Brecht. Here was a whole body of work with which I was familiar, and which used a device of devastating simplicity – the half curtain which he had pioneered with his designer Caspar Neher. I used this in a production of *The Mother* for the National Theatre – a simple white curtain which could traverse the stage horizontally and covered only half the stage height. On it were written the titles of scenes and any information one wanted to give the audience. When following a scene where Pelagea's son had fled over the border to Finland I used the half curtain, Michael Billington wrote

When a charcoal inscribed sheet announced the death of Pelagea's son a woman on my left uttered a devastated sigh; then she leant forward in her seat to discover what effect it would have.

I have never believed a scene is ruined if you know its outcome. In Brecht's plays we find simply a different kind of narration. You look at it not concerned with how it all turns out, but how it could have been different. It is not the destination we are concerned with but the journey. But apart from its use in imparting information, there was another benefit of the half curtain. I knew that it could wipe out the scene just played, and allow during its short passage across the stage the scene behind to be re-set, the actors' positions and predicament to change, a whole set of props and furniture to be struck. It was like those magic slates I used to play with as a child: pull it across and it was clean again. I then started to think about what you could do if you did not use an actual curtain. What could wipe the stage clean and allow me to change scenes simply and quickly without the audience seeing the mechanics of it all?

Then I remembered a workshop with Peter Gill at the Riverside Studios years before. One rainy afternoon in 1978, with about fifteen actors in the room and a vague agenda about staging, he began to talk about Tyrone Guthrie and how he had heard George Devine at the Royal Court describe Guthrie's brilliance in changing scenes. Peter demonstrated a Guthrie way of pulling the audience's attention to one part of the stage while a new character appeared on another part of the stage. An actor was to walk across to the middle of the stage carrying a chair and then sit on it. How could he do this without being seen? He showed us a way to manipulate the audience's gaze.

Two actors played ball across the front of the stage with shouting and laughter and as the ball game finished our eyes followed the actors and the ball off-stage and then came back to rest on-stage. There sat the actor on the chair and we had not noticed how he had got there – our eyes being too taken up with what was happening at the front of the stage. Guthrie would brilliantly manoeuvre large groups on and off and across the stage as if by magic with the use of this very simple principle.

Now I conceived the idea of using an image as a curtain: an image which moved swiftly across the stage to divert the eye. This developed at a later stage into images of characters or events only fleetingly referred to in the text but which I built up and developed as a kind of returning motif. But all the images had to involve a journey through space – to catch the audience's eye or keep it concentrated until the image disappeared and the eye fell back again to characters in a new scene and new place and time. The images cannot be static. They have to be more like slivers of scenes: concentrated, heightened and dynamic.

It is important you accept any 'waiting' actors as an intrinsic part of the mis-en-scene and they should be lit carefully, so that you are not pretending that they are not there but you have a tacit language which declares to the audience they are not for the moment part of the present scene, but they are, as it were, part of the landscape of the piece. Some quite accidental and startling images can occur. It is important that you experiment with different angles of the body and head as the actors sit, stand or lie.

Consider carefully what the actors will sit upon, as your choice of chair can have very far-reaching effects on your staging. At the very least the chair should be light enough to be moved fluidly by one actor. This means that new configurations of chairs can happen swiftly and virtually unseen in the hands of the actor as long as there is another movement going on which more attracts the eye. But the most important aspect of a chair if it is to be really useful to the director and actor is the seat. A chair might be cumbersome to turn in the space but an actor is not, as long as he can slide on the seat of his chair and can go for example from profile to front-facing, effortlessly. An actor simply moving his position on a chair can move unexpectedly into full focus as if a camera had drawn him suddenly into close-up.

A chair is a most potent object on the stage. Chairs assume a strange beauty when arranged symmetrically along the back wall or side of a space. Stacked, they declare the space empty almost indeed in the open air; piled higgledy-piggledy around a small table with a figure standing on top looking into the distance and you have a cliff or a hillside; in a heap they are the barricades of the Russian revolution or the crumbling wall of a derelict building behind which a character can hide. An actor sitting on a chair can turn and reveal his eyes and be suddenly present to the audience; one in profile eyes down can become a distant part of your landscape.

Your aim should be that the action never stops but rolls onward like waves with all the characters, props and furniture found or transformed before the audience's eyes. When you do feel the need to draw out a scene change – while someone is doing a fast change for example or simply because the audience needs to breathe a little and let the change of atmosphere sink in – you are in a position to play with really slowing down a physical movement or a reorganization of objects on stage so that you are conducting the rhythms with sensuality and control as the conductor of an orchestra would.

In *Remembrance of Things Past*, I had eight scenes flow seamlessly across the stage at a tremendous pace. The next scene was laundry women on a river bank. How were we to earn the time to get the actresses changed and ready for the scene? I asked the actor Jim Hooper, playing a waiter at a seafront café, to imagine it was the end of a long shift and to cross the stage very slowly, stacking the last chairs, humming a tune to himself. After the swift pacing of the previous scenes it gave the play breathing space. In the end the lighting designer, Ben Ormerod, lit it like a golden end to a summer's day and it has remained with me as an image of all I love of France and summer nights.

It was the great film director Tarkovsky who described his skill as 'sculpting with time' and fluid staging certainly owes something to the editing techniques in film, for it is the director who often senses where the rhythms must pick up and slow down. Where a group rushes into a scene, or a character moves away slowly calling out the last words of text through a long exit, you can control the images and rhythm imaginatively, directing the audience's eyes to a new scene almost overlapping with the one moving to another part of the stage and settling into stillness or shadow. With the manipulation of waiting figures and the creation of skilful images and intricate moving patterns in the space, you can discover a staging that is dynamic, unexpected and never dogged by repetitive rhythms. Whether it oozes with sensuality is up to you, your actors and your intuitive feel for the movement and interaction of the bodies in the space.

11

SPECIALIST SKILLS

Into any consideration of rehearsal time must come acknowledgement of the role of those with specialist skills: voice, movement, fight and musical directors, lighting and sound designers. These members of your team come to you with years of experience in their special areas and a good director should give them sufficient time to practise their skills. A good fight director is as obsessed with the character's moods and motivations as an actor is. An actor has to know a dance or a song so that it seems effortlessly part of the world of the play.

The first specialist you will work with on a putative production will probably be the designer or scenographer – a European phrase now coming increasingly into use which denotes the area of work involving all the visual aspects of the event on stage. The split between costume and scenic design is one that is more common in the USA than in Europe. I always prefer to work with one person devising the visual world of the play, costumes, set and props so that all more easily coalesce into an integrated whole. The designer and director move the process from the imagination and the directors 'feel' for the play into something not in the mind but on the page in drawings and in a model box with white card shapes – and then on to an exact scale replica of what will be on stage. The designer begins to create the world of the play for all to see, and it is in early sketches, photographs and paintings that you will between you begin to formulate this world, when it is set and where and – most important of all – with what level of abstraction. All the time the good designer is probing the director for a visual clue to how they might imagine or conceive the play and from that clue – an idea, a snippet of music, a photograph, an image described, a sensation analysed, an intellectual construct expounded – the designer takes a pencil and begins to draw. Rooms appear, spaces are hacked out of stages, levels out of spaces, rakes out of levels and slowly an actable space emerges with visual clues to a dramatic world. There is an inevitable interplay between the now and the then and there – we look back at the past through the eyes of the present. We look at the now as if it is unfamiliar and ask ourselves why it is as it is.

It will be through this concretely realized visual world that all the other specialists involved in the production will base their work. The movement director will locate the social world of the period, the dance, the comportment; the lighting designer will find the language of light and shadow, and the music director the sounds. Most importantly, from studying the design they will be able to know whether they are expected to reproduce naturalistic aspects of period or enter a stylized world. Collaborators will look to the director for an articulate definition of the degree of abstraction they may be working in. What is the world of the production – period, modern or a blend of both that says we are in the twenty-first century looking at a story from the past? Specialists need to be guided and not to have to lift a solution out of thin air – although they will try, if they have to. Thence come the murmurs that it is the designer or movement director who is responsible for the production and not the director, who merely oversaw another person's idea. Ideally everyone should work better because the other is there in the collaboration. It is important therefore that you can express your ideas to them; not in the detailed language of their expertise – you do not have to jot down music or know the intricate dance steps of 'Mr Beveridge's Maggot' – but you do have to be able to indicate the style for your evening. Through your work with the designer, basic stylistic decisions will have already been made. If, for example, you are doing a play set in a lodging house in Margate and your design consists of a zinc black box with white light, your lighting designer and composer will respond to this level of abstraction. The music will perhaps be the ripple of the Margate sea electronically transformed into a soundscape, the lighting stark and stylized.

When the designer presents you with a space delineated in a model box and begins to dissect that space with objects – pieces of furniture or abstract levels, entrances, doors, windows or cycloramas – you have to have your facility for looking at top notch, for a bad decision at this stage can affect the whole of the subsequent work, for a chair may be moved but heavy furniture or a scenic piece built over a period of time in a workshop forming an intrinsic part of the set, cannot. Your actors will be stuck with it in all its futility if you do not at this stage subject it to many tests. The basic questions must be: How will it work with the text? Will the text open up to all kinds of possibilities in this space or are you trying to fit the text into the limits of the space? Are you playing a scene in the space given because it needs to be there – it is more expressive when set there – or are you having to place it into the space because you feel you have to use the design? A director together with the designer should subject the space to all the demands the text will make of it.

With many of my designers, we enjoy a detailed examination of the text – often reading the play out aloud – as we manipulate the objects and figures in the model box (and by the way, designers, it is marvellous when the figures resolutely stand up in the model box and are not toppling over every few seconds). I do this, not to decide beforehand how the actors are going to move, but to check there are enough delineated acting areas for them to inhabit, that they have a sufficient multiplicity of choices in the space to respond to the multiplicity of actions they may be playing towards the other characters. These subspaces in a set are of vital significance – the more so when you are working in a non-naturalistic setting where there are swift moving changes of scene, and a new setting has to be suggested with the minimum of means. Or where the actor is in an almost empty space and has to discover the unseen emotional barriers within it.

A young director should always be on the look-out for potential collaborators – the emergent stage and lighting designers, movement and fight directors and composers. A collaborative language is not forged overnight or through one production experience, and your collaborator's expertise will develop alongside yours. You will have your whole careers to create things together. There again it is an incredibly exciting experience to work with specialists who have had more experience than you. The main thing is to feel uncensored in your first explorations, to express your feelings and hunches without embarrassment and to be on the level with your collaborators – neither over-awed nor controlling. A free-flowing dialogue is what you both need.

Looking into the model box at something concrete is a shorthand way into knowing what the director's vision is. So you have to be sure that what everyone else is seeing is what you truly want, that it responds to what you feel viscerally about the play.

For a Shakespeare play, the composer, for instance, looking into the model box might immediately understand that period instruments will be called for. But if there is a mix of periods – Hamlet in a pair of pyjamas, Lear in a twentieth-century military greatcoat – it will be evident immediately in the scenic and costume design and the score may reflect just that ambiguity. It is rare to mix an abstract set and naturalistic music – a sort of post-abstraction – but it does happen, as in the use of a harpsichord in a sci-fi movie. Period music can sometimes sit well in a non-period piece. You could, for example, have an electronic score with samples from period instruments and find it is not too stylistic a jolt. Whatever solution you collaboratively come up with, the world of the play – even if it involves quite startling and new ideas – must somehow be integrated in all its aspects. Ask yourself how naturalistic an evocation of the world of the play is to be created. Are we evoking something authentically historical (if, in fact, that can really exist) or creating a theatrical world of our own that has period references but anachronistic detail: Roman warriors in baseball boots; fairies in Doc Martins? There will be a musical and dance equivalent to this.

Music of and about the play

At an early stage, the composer in reaction to looking at the set may play some music of his own or of another composer, to try to tease out the degree of abstraction needed, for the notion of abstraction may mean different things to different people. There are two categories of music involved in a theatre piece: music *of* the play and music *about* the play. How closely the music of the play corresponds to the playwright's implicit instructions will be a clue to the degree of abstraction. If you look at *Hamlet* for instance there are clearly songs – the gravedigger's and Ophelia's. There is probably music for the dumbshow and this would be partly or wholly provided by the pipes which Hamlet refers to afterwards which the player-musicians were presumably playing; there are references to fanfares and to ordinance – no doubt noted by the scrivener as he watched performances or added by later editors. This could be termed music of the play.

Then there is music about the play: Is there a shimmer of something in the air when the ghost appears? Is there a musical or sound accompaniment to the sword fight? Is the tramp of the army accompanied by a military march?

Traditionally, music about the play has been used to enhance scene changes but this is now altering with the development of a more fluid staging with less formal interruption. Music is used less and less for those scene changes where the lights go down and furniture is moved by stage hands. The music cue is nowadays not so much about the play being chopped up into salami slices but rather about it being pushed forward in an uninterrupted wave. It is for this reason that the last few seconds of music cues need not be resolved musically but cadencially interrupted, so that harmonically they end on a kind of musical question mark rather than a resolution or full stop. And a development from the movies which I often use on stage is to blur the ending of one scene and the beginning of the next by advancing the music cue to the end of the previous scene. All this serves not so much to punctuate a play as to flow it seamlessly forward in an uninterrupted narrative.

Always try to listen to a sound or music cue with reference to the human voice which is to follow it. The sounds should render up the human voice to the audience's ear in its full potency, not leave the actor's voice sounding enervated and thin in comparison to the music that has preceded it. The music should subtly evoke time, place or mood but be so controlled that the human voice is able to vibrate through the space with strength and character as the music fades imperceptibly beneath it.

In opera, the overture often specifies the tone to come or hints at what will be returned to much later. You hear in Bizet's *Carmen* at 7:30 the fanfares of the bullring which you do not hear again until 9:50 – but the return to something already experienced at the outset gives the later moments deep significance. Some directors in an effort to try to help the task of exposition, try to generate a mood or tone by playing music (often loudly) as the audience enters the auditorium. They hope this will engender in the audience the 'right mood'. This is dangerous and always makes me feel there will follow no real trust in the text. An arbitrary music choice – it is often something lifted from a recording – often acts like a blunt instrument and robs the ear of its capacity to really listen to the nuances of speech when the actors take over.

The world you create as a director and the music that accompanies it is most evident when you begin to decide where and why music will come – rather a chicken and egg situation where often the director and composer are waiting for each other to tease out a style for the play. It often seems at this point that you are poised at the very heart of the quest for theatrical language.

If, for instance, you are starting to work on a production of *Romeo and Juliet* as I am at the moment, the music of the play occurs at a party where during a dance Romeo and Juliet meet. I ask myself and my composer: what kind of party, what kind of music, what kind of dance? Then the composer might look to the music about the play and ask if reverberation is something that might be used in the final scenes in the tomb. Should there be off-stage effects – a choir singing, bells tolling?

The dance and social world of the piece will of its nature be intimately connected to, indeed based in, the music. The movement director, working alongside the musical director, may discuss manners and mores or show the director a dance or a set of gestures – she may suggest the actors base their characters on animals, or demonstrate how class may be delineated by body language or how status may be indicated in period reverences. A voice or accent coach may play recordings of relevant material.

What has to emerge from early meetings with your collaborators is an agreed vocabulary. The designer, the composer, the lighting designer, the movement and sound specialists, the combat director all have to integrate their stage language even as each works within his own sphere of speciality. An audience will soon participate with delight in the kind of story-telling means you are going to use, the 'jeu du theatre' – literally the theatre game you are playing – but you have be clear from the outset how the story will be told and not switch narrative convention half way through, otherwise the audience will be confused and irritated. As you ponder these questions your specialists are inching towards a style for the play, probing your reactions.

The area of voice work is probably the most sensitive and complex collaboration of all, since the voice specialist is most nearly concerned with the director's and actors' territory of characterization, emotion, breath and projection. Voice work is never accomplished quickly and the best specialists are extremely careful to try not to interfere with the actor's development of a role. The voice coach may suggest work to help the actors master complex language as well as suggesting how they may be prepared vocally for the theatre space the piece will be played in. A specialist in accents will show the actors how to embody a different culture and where in the mouth unfamiliar sounds are placed. The best voice specialists understand how fundamental breath is not only in the act of speech, but also how intrinsic it is to life itself – it is the first thing that ushers us into life and its cessation will be the last thing to usher us out. *Atem* is the Greek word for breath as well as life. Voice teachers are nearly always the most spiritual of the experts you meet in the theatre because they realize that in working with the voice, they are working with the heart and the deepest part of the human psyche. They have all seen the most spectacular transformations in personality through the release of the breath and the voice. Those that are good are rare and special people and once you find someone in this area you should trust and value them.

One area where the degree of stylization needs to be thought out with great care is when there is a fight or battle on stage. First if a play is not set in its original period there has to be a decision as to what weapons must be used, whether swords or daggers, flick-knives or revolvers. The fight director is extremely skilled at the intricacies of staging combat naturalistically so that the audience can almost believe a blow has landed or a knife been thrust under the rib-cage. Much of this work will consist of making a pretend fight look like a real fight in real time, but when a degree of stylization is called for there often has to be a close collaboration with the composer – as when a fight is rendered in a rhythmical sequence and the composer can supply a quasi-Japanese percussive underscore, or deadly hand-to-hand combat is suggested by three stylized gestures with a dagger, accompanying sound and a sudden silence. A battle sequence impels stylization. Through the centuries the solution has been that there is some kind of evocation of battle off-stage – cannon, shouts, clashing swords – and then an individual is thrown on-stage to bring the conflict into close-up as it were. This may, as you struggle to find the right degree of stylization, sometimes cause conflict too in the rehearsal room, between choreographer and fight director, choreographer and composer. It is the director who has the responsibility to mediate between these areas of expertise and keep everyone quietly working towards the same stage language.

Do not think of the time actors spend with specialists as time off for the director. Of course there are periods where some detail of a dance or a fight can be practised or worked on in another space, when a warm-up is preliminary to the day's work, but the best work is achieved by a proper collaboration – when what the specialist is doing and your feelings about what is needed and how it can all coalesce into a seamless whole, feed into the specialist sessions. If directors call all the movement sessions in the mornings and then habitually arrive when they are finishing, the actors will begin to feel that the work is not central to the director's vision but an adjunct that can be dispensed with. You will not understand how movement or fight or voice work accretes slowly in an actor's characterization. Again and again, I have seen potential for important moments in a production by watching the actors in a movement or fight session – seeing a fleeting image and getting the specialist to build upon it. The best work always comes from proper collaboration with the director's and the specialists' ideas feeding into each other. You must balance well the specialists' need to first teach basic skills, then create more specific input into the production and at the same time maintain a collaborative dialogue in order that their particular sequences seem part of an organic whole. Neither should the atmosphere of the rehearsal room alter when a specialist is working. Sometimes the level of talking in the background goes up when a fight is being rehearsed or music is playing. Prevent this – the specialist needs concentrated attention and quiet just as much as the director does.

Young directors are often nervous that they do not have the specialist language to ask for what they want or imagine a production needs. The fact is you do not need to know what the specialist knows: the how. You only need to convey the why. They can respond to an image, a feeling, a mood, a rough sketch, a magazine picture, a detail from a painting. They are artists too. You do not have to tell lighting directors what you want in terms of lanterns rigged, or calls to the lighting operator. They will want to know the world you are in, the theatrical language you are using – is it naturalistic? Are we in a theatrical world with lighting rig visible? Should the cross-fade be quicker? Then you can talk in images or the emotion you want to evoke, the coolness of the stage or the brutality of a moment and they will give you a creative response. Good lighting designers keep in touch with the production as it starts run-throughs and work on the rig (which lamps are to be put where), the colour palette and the atmosphere of light in an emotional response to what you have evoked in the rehearsal room. The hard graft of organization, of technical skill, of instructing the lighting operator in the split-second timings of cues and the level of the light is firmly their area of expertise. You just have to be expressive: 'Oh, that lighting change has to be much sexier' – and they will give you some alternatives to look at. A warning, give yourself a bit of time when you first look at lighting states on-stage or listen to music cues. It takes time for the eye to adapt to the subtleties of what you are shown or the ear to what you are hearing. Do not panic if in the first instance you cannot tell the difference between them. Your ear and eye will soon adapt.

12

FINAL WORK IN THE
REHEARSAL ROOM

Do not let your anxiety as to whether you have a production with a beginning, a middle and an end rush you into running the play too early in the rehearsal process. You do not need to waste three hours running together scenes that are not ready. It will be time much better spent if you go on working into the details of particular scenes. If you run too early it will be for your sake and not the actors' and they may become downhearted and frustrated at how much remains to be done. Keep patiently working scene by scene, perhaps occasionally letting one scene run on into the next, but do not rush to run-through. The ideal atmosphere for a run-through is when the actors are straining for it like greyhounds in the traps, not full of nervous foreboding.

By now you should have an idea of when you might run the first half, make notes and then run it for a second time before you go through the whole process with the second half. It is sometimes better to run the second half first as you may have been more recently working on that and then go back to some more work on the elements of the first half and run that once it is refreshed in the actors' memory. At each of these run-throughs – be it halves or the whole of the play – allow a generous amount of time for notes.

When taking notes, try to discipline yourself to make what you write intelligible but brief. Notes are like socks; you are always losing one of them. I often see an actor doing the same thing again and again when I am certain I have given a note about an adjustment and the reality is I have never actually given the note. It has got lost in the space between the thought, the pen and the note session. I find I need time to organize my thoughts about a run-through and to make sense of my scrawl by carefully numbering my notes afterwards, separating them on the page and thinking hard about my general conclusions. For this reason, I often take my notes away with me overnight and give them the following morning or work on them through a lunch break so that the note session of the afternoon can be as efficient as possible.

This is where the director and the actors can seriously tackle problems large and small and it is vital that problems should not be addressed theoretically. As each note is given the actors should get to their feet and work the improvement through physically. If there is an adjustment to be made in the speaking of text they should seek it in their scripts and rehearse the speaking of it there and then. This emphasis on taking a note into practice will immediately reveal any shortcoming in the director's note and sink the change into the actors' muscles as well as their minds.

For more major changes, make a list of 'working notes' during the note session and rehearse them methodically one after the other in the space afterwards. A most valuable piece of advice I received as a beginner was to always try to make the play work in the rehearsal room. Moments will not magically transform when you get to the stage because they are well lit, or the actors are magically transformed by their costumes. If dramatic moments do not work in the rehearsal room, they will work even less in performance. If the presence of the audience does work some kind of magic, so much the better. But never, never rely on it.

Working notes take time but it will be time very well spent as it is often here that a real rapport can develop between director and company which will take you through the rigours of the technical week with mutual confidence. The actors will respect your methodical thoroughness and a striving for perfection. I usually allow three hours of working notes after the run-through of an average text but, as the mantra goes, much depends on your instinctive understanding of what is needed and what the actors feel needs adjustment. It can take many more hours. And the actors might need to run the whole thing through again to sink the notes into their muscles. And so on through the various run-throughs.

The final day in the rehearsal room usually coincides with a last run-through. This will hopefully give you an idea of what still remains to be done on a more profound level: of nuance; of characterization, emotional colour, changes in tempo. More prosaic adjustments of positions and staging will be more easily tackled in the technical rehearsals on the actual stage and with the actors in costume. The final run-through in the rehearsal room should give actors a firm emotional and structural base to work from towards performance. In the ensuing stop and start of technical work, they will seem to lose all grasp of the sweep of the play and it will be some days before they can try to return to the concentration and intensity of what they achieved in the final days in the rehearsal room. But they must have a base to return to.

13

TECHNICAL REHEARSALS

Dry technicals

It was from the lighting designer Paul Pyant – a man of visual brilliance, seeming serenity and an amazing collection of cashmere sweaters, who has stood at my side through many extremely difficult technicals – that I learnt the usefulness of the dry technical. Time becomes hideously compressed as the play lurches towards production but a few quiet hours spent with the stage manager, the lighting designer and the musical and sound director before you go into the auditorium can aid a technical rehearsal enormously. I no more want to be tied to notes in a script in the auditorium than I do in the rehearsal room but a dry tech is when, away from the whole paraphernalia of the stage and the many disparate anxieties of those who have been working towards the technical period, you can sit down in a quiet room and calmly discuss and mark down what theatrical events in story-telling, lighting, sound and music will occur at what points in the text. Then at least to some extent you are all singing off the same hymn sheet. Things will change, complexities will occur, doors will not open and scenery will not glide but at least you will have a plan that goes from beginning to end.

Technical rehearsals

The technical rehearsal is where a director must take the helm and make decisions and to a certain extent push the process on as fast as possible. There are many people who have been working in the background who now can see where their work is going to fit in. The designer sees not the model box but the real thing. The actors struggle with props and costumes, dark entrances and twisting staircases, most of which I hope, if you have been vigilant, they have already come to terms with during rehearsal. The wardrobe mistress deep in conversation with the designer sees what needs to be changed in a costume, a colour or a shoe. The music director is setting cue levels and timings and the lighting designer is poring over his plans to find the right palette of light.

Shit, as the saying goes, happens. The sound system crackles, a back drop squeaks, a revolving stage judders. The production manager and the crew, drills in hand, hammers at the ready, make adjustments and come up with solutions – some immediately, some just in time in the hours before first night. The actors stand around, go over and over two or three lines until their costumes hurt them and their make-up cakes and cracks. Actresses red-eyed with fatigue stare at you through lashes that cannot be their own, actors sweat until their wrinkles run and their moustaches slip. Calm people get cross and cross people weep. And all the time, directors wonder where the play has gone in the mass of detail as around them maybe as many as fifty or a hundred people jostle for decisions and attention.

This is the time to use that wartime expression that so helped the British: keep calm and carry on. Do not give in to the temptation to not really get something right because you are worried about time or exhausted or depressed. 'Genius', said Thomas Carlyle, 'lies in the infinite capacity for taking pains' – and as far as I am concerned, so does common or garden craftsmanship. On the other hand, you must learn to judge when a problem can be left for a later solution – a special light to be rigged in a break, a costume altered overnight to aid a quick change, a complicated scene change worked on later in previews.

Do not hesitate to come up with solutions even though they may seem naive. In *Gawain*, we came late in a rehearsal upon a seemingly insurmountable problem. Gawain had to exit but his path had to cross a void where a section of the stage had been lowered and could not be raised again in time. Next morning I suggested a most mundane and clumsy solution I had thought of during the night – and luckily Alison Chitty had thought along the same lines. A plank of wood was thrown across the gap by a stage hand – obscured by a swirl of activity on stage I quickly invented – and Gawain made his way across this rough bridge. Similarly when the 'headless body' (played by an actress who reached precisely to the Green Knight's shoulders) found herself too small to mount the horse, I invented another diversion and we managed to get a ladder on and off stage again without anyone seeing. Even during the first night, when I noticed that the great door in the set had stuck ajar and knew that this would lead to later dire complications, I rose from my seat and went backstage in evening dress, saw a singer in Knight's armour watching terrified from the wings and told him to go on-stage and close it. It is not a question of what you can do but of what must be done. Take up the responsibility to solve problems: do not be defeated by them.

Try to give each decision and each member of the team your full attention as you turn from one to the other. Make sure you have taken time to go to the wardrobe during rehearsals and just said hello and looked at what the seamstresses are doing. Know the name of the wardrobe assistant. Know who the carpenter is. Walk down to the stage one morning and introduce yourself to the crew. I did this once at the Royal Opera House Covent Garden during an early morning change-over of set and they could not have been more astonished if the Queen had suddenly arrived – hardly any directors had ever visited them on stage, let alone one who was a young woman. As more and more people come into the process do not let the group around you become amorphous, keep having real dialogue, on the level and with the individual.

When the technical rehearsal starts, the stage crew and technical teams are waiting to see how the director is going to handle it all. This was especially daunting at the beginning of my career when, in some of the theatres I worked in, no woman had run technicals before and everyone dreaded some 'dithering female' who could not exercise technical control. For this reason, I soon decided to work out carefully what I wanted to happen in the first minutes – when the music should begin, when the houselights started to fade, how long the cross fade should take, the quality of the first lighting cues, how the first event on-stage should proceed. And I tried to achieve it quickly and to the very best of my ability. I made clear decisions in a calm and confident voice and then I said the magic words 'Let's go on', even if secretly I guessed that I would come back at a later stage and finesse something. This reassures the technical staff, everyone feels the rehearsal will progress at a decent rate and their relief calms me down.

At the end of a technical rehearsal, which in some theatres may have lasted for days, go on stage and thank the actors and turn to the auditorium and thank everyone else who has sat there in the dark for fourteen hours. Then go home and go to sleep. You will need all the rest you can for the exigencies of the next task: having to let the actors find the play again without any interruption. A director's bed though is not a bed of roses, because almost without exception, directors find the text of the play swirling through their sleep in endless convoluted anxious currents. The only solution I have ever found is to treat it like an illness and take something to make me sleep without these dreams which leave me exhausted and fretful. Not a state in which to face dress rehearsals.

126

Dress rehearsals

The dress rehearsal is where the actors begin to get hold of the play and make the telling of it their own. Here, in the dark of the auditorium, you will begin to sense what it is you have together come up with. You are looking at all the technical details – lighting, costume, scene transformation – and with you are all the experts in this field looking with a critical eye at their part in the proceedings too. Keep on keeping calm and carrying on, noting the myriad details that need adjusting. As in run-throughs in the rehearsal room, many details will iron themselves out as the calling of cues and the smoothness of changes improve with practice. You will also be sensing the arc of the play only dimly perceived through the mist of tiny mis-timings and unfamiliar practicalities. Keep an eye on all this – the actors will be keen to get the technical operation of the play smooth as quickly as possible and will begin to bring in their own suggestions and solutions – and also try to concentrate as much as possible on the actors and their performances. They will be hungry for the best, most sensitive, articulate and detailed notes you can muster because if things go well you will all begin to sense something that is more than the sum of its parts – group spirit. It is this that will have the power to inspire and move the group it was all intended for: the audience. And the audience in turn will have an almost magical power to teach you and your actors what the play is.

If you want to re-stage a scene change or some complicated technical manoeuvre, now is the time to pre-plan. This is where when I get home, I do what I have avoided doing all through rehearsal. I get out a tray, label spice jars with actors names and plan an entire sequence in detail and make sure I know it off by heart. Then when you go into next day's rehearsal with all the appropriate technicians present, and the actors saving their energies for a dress rehearsal or preview, you will have a definite plan of action which you can alter and perfect as you work, but which must be rehearsed calmly and quickly so that everyone has full confidence in it for the evening. It is sometimes a better use of time to explain the whole thing to the technicians first and call the actors later to fit them in. At this point, I like to run a sequence not so that everyone can get it right but so that no-one can get it wrong.

14

THE FINAL INGREDIENT:
THE AUDIENCE

From dress rehearsal onwards the actors should be encouraged to think about serving the play up to the audience: opening it out to the house and embracing this new and most important group of participants in the process, to listen carefully to their responses and to feel the currents and eddies of emotion they give off. The minutest variation in clarity or timing, a pause, a turn or a look can draw an audience in or leave them out in the cold, unresponsive and restless. Each audience is unique and takes its particular time to settle, to laugh, to become enthralled, to lose interest; but here is the last vital ingredient in the mix. Move around the theatre as the performance proceeds and study the audience – how they breathe, look, laugh, where they become restless, look at the programme, study the ceiling.

Allow the audiences to teach you and your actors about the play. You will suddenly realize there are unnecessary longueurs, that the plot is not clear, a certain word is not landing cleanly, a character fails to be as moving as they should be, that a bit of staging obscures the narrative drive. It is only when the audience is there with that special group concentration and atmosphere they bring to a room that things suddenly become blindingly obvious which did not occur to you or the actors in the rehearsal room.

When I did a production of Brecht's *The Resistible Rise of Arturo Ui* at the Olivier Theatre in London, the audience failed to respond to a sequence based on the Reichstag fire, where a group of gangsters cynically commit arson in order to spread panic and justify a witch-hunt. I re-rehearsed in preview so that the text and the staging were as clear as we could make them. Still no response. Nicholas Wright, a National Theatre colleague and playwright, suggested the audience just could not understand, despite the text and my having had the gasoline cans painted bright red, that the gangsters indeed had gasoline in their hands. I had *gasoline: danger* painted in large white letters on the cans and at last the audience responded to the dark comedy of the moment.

I should warn young directors too of something that often occurs at last preview or first night – anyway when it is far too late to make alterations. You settle into your seat, the lights go up and you suddenly realize you should have approached the play in a completely different way and a new vision of it falls into your mind. This is similar to the moment when someone tells you that if they had done it, they would have done it differently. You have to remind yourself that you have actually brought something into existence – usually something not insubstantial – and that it actually exists unlike your alternative or a colleague's theory and that this – the forging of something out of nothing – is an achievement all of it own.

As opening night looms nearer, you should try to give fewer and fewer notes. If the rehearsal has been properly conducted, from the right basis, the production will have a life of its own which is thoroughly grounded in the text and with – dare I employ this overused word – an organic nature of its own which will bloom in the actors' hands. The director at this point should be doing less and less, not more and more. Listen to the problems the actors bring you and be ready with suggestions or simple reassurance and keep tightening up the nuts and bolts of the complex mechanism that is the play on the stage. There is a moment usually after first previews, when you get what I call 'family notes'. The actors react with extreme sensitivity to what their near and dear ones have to say about the play, the production and more particularly their performance. You have to use your judgement as to what is useful, what reflects your own instincts and what you have sensed yourself from audience reaction. Proceed calmly, listen carefully to what the actors report but do not be over-reactive. In the end it will not reassure the actors at all if you are 'a feather for every wind that blows'. Hold on to your vision because, for good or ill, it has animated you throughout all the pre-production preparation and the rehearsal period. It has helped you inspire your production team, and being seen to vacillate will unnerve your actors.

However, have the courage of your convictions if, in experiencing the arc of the play in the presence of an audience, you genuinely realize something must be massively changed. Change it but plan well. Take the actors and technicians into your confidence. Warn them that it will be lots of work, and get on with it swiftly, confidently and with as much rehearsal and as many run-throughs as you can devise. If your courage fails you at this point, you will always regret it. I changed the order of the first four scenes of *The Revenger's Tragedy* at Stratford in final previews and had to take the company and the technical crew with me despite their misgivings. And I have never regretted it.

By first night the actors are not quite with you when you meet before the performance: they are like the mortally ill. They have their eyes on the horizon. The journey they are setting out on will not include you. The actors have a new guide – their audience. They are in their true element – the theatre. You are not there with them on a podium like a conductor. They are fast leaving you behind. The group with luck is coalescing. They have an unspoken camaraderie you will not be a part of. They will greet you warmly when you visit the dressing room after shows, they will listen politely to notes, they will ask advice but essentially, they will have left you behind.

And then sometimes there is a particular kind of magic by which an actor leaves you totally, breathlessly behind. You are present when a unique display of talent is ushered into the theatre. You will suddenly realize that a particular actor by an almost uncanny transference of thought and feeling between stage and onlookers has the audience completely under their sway. Some actors are transformed by the audience's presence as if they imbibe some special energy. They become more alive, more vivid, more themselves than they ever are in ordinary life. They are the naturals; they 'have it for nothing'. You can sense it straight away even in an inexperienced actor giving an as yet rough performance: it is as if when they enter the stage they are suddenly in their natural element like a fish in water. Moments like this are rare but they are inestimable. These actors have a great deal to teach the director about the intangibles of the craft and of the existence of that great mystery: talent. You will never be able to explain it, or to create it where it does not exist – your response can only be to thank God or the Fates or an accident of nature that you were born at that moment in time where you were witness to it.

Visiting your production, you will see that it has subtly grown away from you. You will stand at the back of the auditorium and see taking place, if all goes well, a love affair between spectator and player from which you are excluded. The production ideally should not be a baby that has to be cosseted and checked at every turn. It should have a life of its own. This means you have to a great extent let go of it, and trust that the work you have done will permeate its every development. Then there is the dread and disappointment of something not quite achieved. Success is oddly more difficult to get over than failure. It can make the days after the show has gone on in the theatre, exhausted, forlorn and flat. You are lonely. You are depleted. You may pine for the laughter of the rehearsal room, for the camaraderie of the technical team. Then again, you may breathe a sigh of relief and think 'never again'. There is only one solution: open the fresh first page of a new play and say to yourself in as confident a voice as you can muster, 'Let's go on.'

Part 3

DIRECTING: THE KWOTH

15

A FIGURE IN THE DISTANCE

As I was growing up in Birmingham in the early 1950s in a city full of bomb sites, coal shortages and rationing, I knew who had lost the war – we had. It was the age of austerity. Later I would describe it as 'all cold brown linoleum'. How could people talk of victory?

But slowly it dawned on me, there had been a victory – for me, at least. In a short time, there were new baby clinics where they gave out free orange juice and checked on my weight and my height, a new infants school in Stanville Road where we drank a third of a pint of free milk every morning. My mother, down to her last penny, drew family allowance each week from the Post Office and breathed with relief that she had money in her purse for another few days and all the men in my neighbourhood were in jobs – my father building cars in the day and working as a bookies' clerk at the dog tracks at night. My victory was gained not in Berlin but from all those men and women sickened by the Depression who on their return from fighting cast their vote for a Labour government and a new kind of socialized Britain.

What I did not yet realize was that the Education Act of 1944 was to give me my passport out of Birmingham – to the grammar school and the university and away from the fate of past generations of Trevis's. It would eventually separate me from my class and all that was familiar in my childhood until all that would remain between me and my father would be in the poet Tony Harrison's words 'not the thirty or so years, but books, books, books'. When I finally got to describe life with my father – to a psychotherapist in Hampstead in the late 1970s – I expected him not to believe it. I almost did not believe it myself. It was like the worst kind of depressing kitchen-sink drama.

At base, there was – and this is where Marx seemed to me later to bring me my first relieved understanding of it – a quite simple economic exploitation at work. My father ruled the household despotically and he caught my mother and thus us, the children, in a double bind. He forbade my mother to leave the house to work and at the same time left her desperate for money. He gave her what he called in a nice term her 'wages' at the end of the week and throughout much of my adolescence this was in the region of £7. This figure – £7 – lurked painfully in my mind for years and when I finally was able to speak those words – £7 a week – a torrent of almost inconsolable sobbing accompanied it. It was the only money my father would ever give my mother and from that she had to feed, house, clothe, pay bus fares for, buy school uniform for, three growing children. She had to pay the heating bills, rent and everything for the house – curtains, sheets, tea towels. She had to buy her own clothes and anything personal that she needed.

At some point in the past (when I was a baby) she had got into a position whereby before the Friday payout, she had 'borrowed' from the next week's amount. My father would solemnly, slowly, sadistically count out her money onto the kitchen table – minus her debt. He was meticulous down to the last penny. This meant that she simply never had enough 'wages' on a Friday to last her the week and throughout my childhood, worry about money consumed her.

There would sometimes be a terrible moment when on a Wednesday or Thursday, she would ask him nervous and sweaty handed for a 'loan'. Sometimes he would grudgingly give it. Sometimes he would rage and threaten. You could never predict his mood. She would cry when he was out of the house, and pointing to my feet she would wail 'and you need a new pair of shoes' and I would for weeks try to walk lightly to put off the dreaded day when she would have to find the money for a new pair. She tried to buy us shoes only once a year (through a credit firm called The Provident which allowed you credit in special shops and charged 10% for the privilege) and when I got a new pair I would put them near my pillow so that I could awake to the sheer shining joy of them next morning – a thing I was only able to stop doing once I had married and my husband persuaded me they would not go away overnight if I put them in a wardrobe. She managed the children's food as cheaply as she could but my father had expensive tastes. He liked steak and halibut – and hadn't he paid for it? So this she had to provide. I soon learnt the contours of shame. Walking up the road to the butcher's shop with a note asking for 'strap' – credit on an account long overdue and which the butcher would have refused unless a child were handing over the scribbled note – sitting in the dark with my mother silent while the tradesmen knocked at the door for payment and we had to pretend to be out. The worst terror came when we avoided the rent man, for that my mother would explain might mean eviction. All the time my father lived his life – seven clean white shirts a week for his nightly outings, suits and overcoats tailored for him by Mr Basovitch on the Bristol Rod – the first Jewish name I ever heard – a set of golf clubs, the car, the racetrack and the boxing ring – he was a referee of amateur boxing and later a judge. He knew how to wield the iron fist with which he ruled the house. Home from the track, he would sometimes count slowly a handful of notes and then unfold the big white fivers and smooth them out with satisfaction: but none of this money came to us.

Then my mother embarked on a choice which held such terrors for me I could hardly breathe: she decided to go to work secretly. If he had found out, I am certain he would have murdered her. The first occasion was when a farmer from the Warwickshire countryside came down the street one morning recruiting day labourers for potato picking. The next day, my father safely at his workplace, my mother dressed in an old coat and a headscarf climbed up into the back of an open truck with a group of neighbours and went off to pick potatoes. She came back at four o'clock that afternoon, cash in her pocket, triumphant though her hands were raw and her back in agony. This lasted for a week and every day she had to hide her hands and try to walk normally in front of my father. Women herded into the back of a truck, my mother dicing with danger in this subterfuge, the image of her clinging on to the rattling sides of the vehicle being taken away from me: I did not need the grainy documentaries about transportation in the Second World War to wring my heart – post-war Birmingham did it already.

Later she worked as a cleaner in middle-class Solihull, walking the four miles there and back to save the bus fare, in a series of detached mock-Tudor houses set back in leafy roads. I would be taken with her in the school holidays and sent to play with the children of the house. Once we played at boarding school in the garage and I dreamed afterwards of the heaven it would be if only I could escape to a school. And all the time, I dreaded her being found out.

Once, unable to find a pair of socks that he liked, I had witnessed my father take a room apart – my mother haggard and white of face – as cupboard contents flew against the walls. One night I was awoken by the sound of him raging at my mother in the bedroom and heard him go down the stairs as my brother called goodbye to his friends in the street, and wait behind the door. He lashed out at the eighteen-year-old with punches. His crime? He had bought a pair of drain-pipe trousers with his first wages and my father had seen them hanging over a chair and had decided they were forbidden. He would intone to me: 'If you dare leave this house I will find you wherever you are and break your back.'

Litz Pisk saw my fear of this threat lurking in my shoulders and spine years afterwards and as I released it, my emotions poured out. In time my brothers left school and started to work, giving my mother money from their wages each week. They paid me too for ironing – 6d a shirt – for they each got through at least seven clean shirts a week.

As I grew older and went to the grammar school, the horror of my father's control spread to me. But for me, he retained a special kind of spite. I was bright, articulate, always reading, full of opinion, backed up by facts: it drove him to a frenzy. He called discussion 'answering back', and smacked me across the head for it. I knew already that my only passport out of what I called Birmingham but which really meant that house, was education and getting that passport meant working for three hours every night. His special pleasure was to forbid the use of a one-bar fire in my bedroom as it 'wasted' electricity. My room, with an exposed outer wall facing north-east, was glacial and through the winter I would work steadily every evening dressed in my homework outfit: duffel coat, hood up, gloves and a scarf so that I could have silence and space. I loved school. I loved to learn. I loved to read. Night after night I slogged through Cicero's *Philippics*, essays on *Wuthering Heights* and irregular French verbs. When I went to the school library I would look at the shelves and feel a strange sensation in my stomach. Later I realized what it was: hunger, spiritual hunger. I wanted to read every single book. Home from school on winter evenings, I would find my mother sitting in the dark in front of the fire – she loved firelight. We would sit together, talk quietly and drink tea. And then I would hear my father's key in the door and escape to my room so as not to witness his bullying and her abjection. She was terrified of him and from her I learnt terror too.

But by then I was terrified of the biggest baddest father of them all which was going to come inevitably one day and drag me off: death. I first realized this one dark night when my father left me in the back of his van on his way back from a day at the races when he stopped off at a country pub to drink with friends. Children were not allowed in bars and were left in the car park with a packet of crisps and a glass of lemonade. I was about eight years old and experienced an indescribable terror and screamed and screamed to the point of faintness but no-one heard. This sometimes overwhelming, sudden deluge of terror at the thought of no longer existing has afflicted me all my life: I scream or barely stifle a scream and feel the world spinning and my heart bursting and I know no-one can save me from it. At the same time, this moment marked the

138

beginning of my creativity. From this very young age I felt in a race with eternity. Time's winged chariot is always at my heels. I had to express myself and to have witnesses too or else my life would be worthless. Every mark on blank paper, every moment of my theatre pieces is a living defiance of my mortality. It made me driven. There is thus a special irony in my work being in the theatre. For the very nature of the theatre is its transience: once over, you can never get it back. Again and again you rehearse mortality. In the beauty of a given moment lies the poignancy of it not being captured for the future: it is only in the now and for those witnessing it in the moment, then it is gone. It is 'in a nette to catch the wind'.[1]

> The moving Finger writes; and, having writ,
> Moves on: nor all thy Piety nor Wit
> Shall lure it back to cancel half a Line,
> Nor all thy Tears wash out a Word of it[2]

My father wrote in his beautiful handwriting in the first page of my autograph book. And of course there was another side to this father of mine. Hatred is never the problem. A good strong gust of hate is energizing and intoxicating. I overcame stage-fright by standing in the wings and summoning up sheer hatred of the audience who caused the fear in me. No. The problem is always love. As much as I hated and feared my father, I loved him too. He read voraciously like me and he had learned a lot of poetry by heart. His especial love was Shakespeare and I owe to him my joy in the spoken word. He had what his Irish mother called the gift of the gab, always able to talk his way out of scrapes and he was charming – I see him now in a bar, glass of gin in hand surrounded by friends, embarked on a story, with the smoke from his cigarette blown in a perfect smoke-ring floating above his handsome face, everyone around him laughing. He was what is called 'black Irish' – with Mediterranean good looks inherited, it is said, from the Spanish sailors cast ashore on the Irish coast after the wreck of the Armada: thick black hair brilliantined back, high cheekbones and a full beautiful mouth.

He was the last of his mother's eleven children and sister-reared. My aunt Winnie, sixteen years his senior, whose task it was to care for him from a baby, loved him passionately all her life and flew ever to his defence. He was a very clever schoolboy, passing into the grammar school on a scholarship. He was forced to leave at fifteen by the death from throat cancer of his father. Even with a scholarship, the family could not afford the uniform and the books. Later, I attended the same grammar school and an elderly teacher told me my father had been the most talented mathematician he had ever taught and it was a tragedy his schooling had been cut short. Therein, no doubt, lay his envious rage towards me.

In the summer, my father would drive into the countryside to fish or watch cricket and with him I learnt to love the contours and hedgerows of Shakespeare's Warwickshire: 'I know a bank whereon the wild thyme blows.'[3] Standing on the opposite bank of the Avon, looking over to the Shakespeare Memorial Theatre, he told me once that to work there was considered the greatest honour in the theatre and that any actor would pay to walk on the stage. He did not live to see me work there. He died at the age of fifty-two of cancer. Almost his last act was to write a poem. I was glad he had died, exultant like a figure in a Greek tragedy, and at his funeral wore a dress of white satin. By this time my parents had had a late baby and she was then four years old, sitting on a swing in the garden as the mourners came into the house stuffing, Irish-fashion, banknotes down the side of the sofa for my mother to find later. Told that he had gone to heaven and that it was better that way, my sister sang happily at the top of her voice, 'Daddy's gone to heaven. Hooray, hooray, hooray.' I wanted to sing with her. My mourning took a long time to come and when I cried at last it was for the whole damn mess, not for him.

However, his ghostly figure is almost always there in my work. That image of a figure receding into the depth of the space – or even more miraculously, turning and slowly emerging from the darkness to speak – is surely one of the most simple but thrilling of images the theatre has to offer. When an actor enters solitary into the space and turning, begins to speak to me, I am returned to that windy day of my childhood and I am not left behind. My love is redeemed.

16

MY SALVATION

I was fourteen when I discovered the theatre. An eccentric older girl from school, Hester Bolton, whose communist mother had insisted on state education, somehow sensing I was a fellow spirit, stopped me on the stairs one day and asked me if I wanted to join a youth group being formed in the city centre at an amateur theatre called the Crescent. This was a well-established organization with high production standards despite its amateur status, with a lovely little dilapidated theatre with red plush seats and backstage rehearsal rooms stacked with old furniture and beyond, rickety staircases leading to offices and workrooms. It smelled of theatre – damp, paint, sweat and a lingering whiff of powder and perfume. There I joined a group rehearsing an adaptation of *Pride and Prejudice* and eventually played Lydia, the younger daughter who elopes with an unsuitable man.

Kids from all over the city came to the Crescent and I got to know a much more socially mixed group than I had ever before encountered. Through a chance invitation from one of them, I made my way one early evening to a house across the city. It lay beyond an imposing gateway at the end of a long, twisting drive: an Edwardian mansion of peeling stucco in five acres of garden with a lake and a bluebell wood. That first evening I could see nothing but its looming outline, and the branches overhead moving in the wind. The stones of the driveway crunched under my feet and there was a smell of damp leaves and pine needles. A light shining in a courtyard to the back of the house led me to a coach house, an arched window, a blur of candlelight. I rang the bell and stepped through the doorway into a small hall leading to a dining room. Dinner was over and among the mess of glasses and bottles on the table sat a coffee pot, its silver reflected in the mahogany surface. I was ushered to a seat and handed a tiny jade green cup of black coffee with a silver spoon nestling in its brilliant saucer. I thought I had never seen anything more beautiful. A grey haired man with glasses and a spotted bow-tie, turned to me smiling and said 'So what are you reading?' 'The biography of a poet called Rupert Brooke', I said. 'I was at Cambridge with Rupert', the stranger replied.

I had met my salvation.

Philip Sargant Florence was an eminent economist recently retired from Birmingham University. His mother, Mary Sargant, was an English painter and had defied Victorian convention to study art in Paris where she had met his American father Henry Smythe who was training as an opera singer. His career as a singer did not prosper despite his changing his name from Smythe to Florence which he imagined would be more Italianate. They married and, returning to America, quickly had two children, Philip and his sister Alix, a year his junior.

On a seaside outing one day in New Jersey, with the two children on the beach, Mary witnessed her young husband drown. Philip suspected later his father's death was less an accident than suicide, but there was no way of knowing. Mary, a young widow in a strange country, realized she must make her home in England but dreaded a return to the confines of her family – the worst kind of haute bourgeoisie was how Philip described them. So his mother insisted on establishing her own household in a house on Marlowe Common where there was a well-established artists' colony. Here she brought her children up according to her own modern beliefs: earth-closet toilets, home-baked bread, a vegetarian diet and open-toed sandals. She built herself a studio and painted relentlessly – a painting of Philip and his sister Alix riding on the Common on a donkey is still stored away somewhere in the basement rooms of the Tate Gallery in London. Unconventional all her life, she made an exception on the subject of her son's education, took advice from her brothers and Philip was eventually dispatched to Rugby School. He loathed it. He had been brought up in a household of women, detested sports and did not believe in God. Thomas Arnold's regime of Muscular Christianity at Rugby school was anathema to him. He hated the old-fashioned curriculum which concentrated mainly on the Classics, and with a retentive memory for dates and details, he wrote an exam question on the Battle of Waterloo and won a scholarship to Caius College, Cambridge to study history.

He soon developed an interest in economics, adored his brilliant tutor, later colleague, Maynard Keynes and joined a university society called the Heretics. Most of his young contemporaries at Cambridge died in the war that soon followed – Rupert Brooke, for one. Had Philip not been a American citizen, he would have been forced to declare himself a pacifist as many of his London friends did, for by now his sister had joined him in Cambridge after her education at Bedales and the Slade School and introduced him to her circle – friends like Dora Carrington from the Slade and the famously beautiful four Olivier sisters, one of whom, Noel, was engaged to Rupert Brooke – the Neo-Pagans Virginia Woolf called them. Philip's sister later moved to Vienna to be analysed by Freud, married James Strachey, Freud's English translator and started practising as a psychoanalyst in Gordon Square, Bloomsbury. Thus, Philip came into the orbit of the Bloomsbury group.

In 1915, he went to New York to Columbia University and began his first major book – an analysis of American industry – and was asked by the Cambridge philosopher and pacifist, Bertrand Russell, to deliver a letter to the headquarters of the Womens' Peace Movement. Lella Secor, a young journalist from Spokane, Washington was manning the office on the day he delivered the letter and he took her to coffee in Greenwich village. She had red hair, pale blue eyes and took his arm, chatting easily as they walked down the street. He had never met a woman like this before. He fell totally in love with her. They were married in 1917 and until her death he celebrated, with presents and general rejoicing, the day he met her, the day she accepted his proposal and the day they were married.

This then was the man who invited me to have tea with him the following Friday and lent me a copy of Rupert Brooke's 1911 poems with Rupert's own corrections in them. He had come to Philip's room at Caius, handed him a copy and put a line through one of the titles and written 'Lust' where the publishers had printed 'Libido'. Philip became, along with all the members of his extended household, quite simply a lifeline to me. At tea in his study, seated before the spluttering gas fire, he offered at once any book from his shelves I wanted to read. 'Think of me as your lending library', he said. But it was not only books he gave me. He ushered me into a different world. Highfield, his eccentric and most beautiful house, was a marvel. I was not the first waif and stray to find comfort there. The great hallway with its coloured tiles and sweeping staircase was decorated on every surface – doors and ceiling too – with scenes from Stravinsky's opera *Petrushka* by the artist Joan Souter-Robinson who had once come for the weekend and stayed for months. Upstairs an enormous gold-framed mirror covering half the bedroom wall had been left there by one of the many Jewish refugees they had housed in the 1930s. How had he brought it with him?

Customs of New York – first name terms, good coffee mid-morning and strong cocktails at five (I learnt to make a mean martini) prevailed. But most important was, of course, the spirit of the place. It was civilized –

conversation, reasoned argument, liberal ideas, aesthetic judgement, style, elegance: all these I learned from Highfield and its world and its visitors. And I drank it in – every social nuance, turn of phrase, original idea, train of argument. A journalist and campaigner to keep America out of the First World War, Lella had then turned her attention to women's rights and birth control. She contacted Gregory Pincus[1] after birth control trials in Puerto Rico and introduced the contraceptive pill into Britain for the first time and from her I learned to look towards a vast horizon of freedom – sexual, economic and social.

The house was full of people – a Belgian astrophysicist and his ageing mother in the two attic apartments; a young woman, who washed the dishes in exchange for accommodation, with her husband and baby in rooms behind the kitchen; Mr Hussey, the gardener, in the basement, learning French in his retirement; and Gilbert Walker the economist in the coach-house, where previous occupants had included the poets Louis MacNeice and Julian Bell – son of the painter Vanessa Bell – later killed in the Spanish Civil War. It was with Walker's son, David, that I began my first love affair. The Florences, of course, had money but how they chose to use it was revelatory. They drove old cars until they were beyond repair, were not in the least interested in fashion or the new. Things were beloved because they were old and worn. What was of real value was food, gin, books and most of all beauty. And the beauty intoxicated me: tall French windows in all the downstairs rooms led to a charming curved veranda which in turn gave onto on one side a rose garden and below a lawn sweeping down to a lake overhung with a willow. Beyond the lake lay a small wood and at one side an arched folly rescued from a demolished church. Later when I was away working in the theatre, Philip would dig up a tiny clump of the first snowdrops and send them to me by post, wrapped in a scrap of damp newspaper, to remind me of that beloved garden. In the house, there were books everywhere, worn wooden floors, log fires, an old grand piano, colour, light and congeniality.

But most important of all – beyond the relief of it all, the sense of a kind of undemanding, easy love, the unsparing help, the genuine interest in me and my ideas – was my colossal sense of culture shock, for I saw culture and class dispassionately for the first time. Highfield and my home existed as it were side by side and yet worlds apart. I could analyse the rites and rituals of both and, at the same time, practise my skill as a participating actor in this new culture. I decided I wanted to be on the margin, an observer, an analyst of society not dragged down blindly into its control. I saw that you could break away, that you could make yourself over, that you could take a subculture and examine it intellectually, that there was a way of analysing your own deepest responses, of finding the causes of attitude and prejudice, of fear and resentment, of violence and frustration: that my background was explicable and, most of all, escapable. The culture shock of the theatre and Highfield collided and I felt with certainty I would spend my life putting society in all its variety onto a stage and so deprive it for the rest of my life of its power to imprison me.

17

I BECAME A DIRECTOR
ONE WEEKEND

One summer evening I found myself walking up the Portobello Road in London and miserably taking stock of my life. I was dirt poor, unhappy in love, and too thin. I was a professional actress. Nancy Mitford, once asked by her mother to write a notional household budget for a year, devoted all but a pound of it to flowers. I had a similar tendency, if less money. If I had £15 in my purse for the week, I would calculate: taxis £12.00. The balance covered a large bag of muesli, milk and bread for the week. I felt life would not be worth living if, on my way to auditions or coming back late from the theatre, I had to wait for buses or descend to the underground burdened with shoes for walking and heavy coats in case of rain. It had to be faced. I was stony broke and the nervous tension of my life as an actress was wearing me down. I preferred to ward off depression rather than eat a square meal. All my life people had decided I was promising and I knew that at nearly thirty I ought to start delivering on that promise. This was not a rehearsal. It was my life and it was dribbling away. I was highly educated with absolutely no ordinary marketable skills. I didn't type, I couldn't drive and I was a hopeless waitress.

And then I had a totally new and radical thought. What if I gave up being an actress? That was ridiculous. Acting was almost the only thing in life that gave me unalloyed happiness. I had, amongst all my other doubts, never doubted that. But then another thought occurred to me: what if it were not acting per se but the theatre I loved? And suddenly, there on a London street, with the moon rising and the litter of the market stalls in the gutters, I knew and I knew completely and irrevocably I wanted to be a director. A simple thing, but hard to do. I was filled with a kind of vertigo. There were lots of women in the theatre but they were not directors. They were costume designers, stage managers, casting directors: female helpmates. Neurasthenic, blonde actresses in their late twenties – girls like me – did not become directors. So I went back home, sat down and waited for the proverbial cooked chicken to fly through the window. Nothing happened, of course.

Weeks later, I finally told a fellow actor the conclusion I had reached. 'I think I am a director', I said. He in turn mentioned the conversation to the director Peter Gill who broached the subject with me over a cup of tea at the Riverside Studios where I attended workshops for actors.

'You have decided me', he said. 'I am going to organize a workshop for young directors one weekend soon. Would you like to come?'

'Trouble is, Peter', I said, 'I am not a young director. I just think I want to be one.'

'That is precisely why you must come to my workshop', he replied. 'If you spend the weekend saying you are a director, by Monday you will be one. Or', he added wryly, 'as much of one as most other directors.'

Underneath this levity was a serious analysis. Directors had not traditionally been trained, especially in Great Britain. They had simply come about. So I went to the weekend, met about ten young directors – some of whom are now busy working in the theatre and television – and woke up on Monday morning with a focus.

Peter had told me to start to search for a new play that I really liked, buy the rights to it and persuade a theatre to put it on. He even pointed me in the direction of the Riverside bar. He thought a young playwright sitting in there might know of a new play. Paul Kember had just written *Not Quite Jerusalem* and said he knew a playwright, Shaun Lawton, living in Berlin, who had written a vast, sprawling five-act play set among Elvis-loving unemployed youths in Newcastle. He thought it had real passion in it but needed masses of re-organization and all the theatres he'd shown it to appeared frightened of it. It was called *Desperado Corner.*

By Thursday, I had a copy in my hand, borrowed £100 and bought the rights to it. Then I set about trying to cut it into a manageable length and cast size, having talked over the phone to the writer Shaun who had come to a creative impasse with it and needed someone else to try to move it forward. 'It's been rattling around readers and agents for two years', he said, 'and I don't know any more what to do with it – try something and come to Berlin and we'll look at it together.' Berlin? I couldn't afford the fare. But getting to Berlin became top of my agenda.

Then a small part in a movie came up. I was cast to play a Polish resistance fighter in the Warsaw ghetto – a chance to cash in on my low weight and my desperation. It was filming near Wroclaw in Poland and I asked the casting director if my airfare could be paid to me directly and I could make my own travel plans. 'I am directing now,' I said to her firmly 'and I need to stop in Berlin on my way back.' I bought a train ticket to Wroclaw, returning via Warsaw to Berlin. When the train drew into its terminus, I realized I was the wrong side of the Berlin Wall. I asked an old gentleman on the platform pathetically where the West was. He pointed me to some low buildings across what looked like an old bomb site, I scuttled through the checkpoint and two days later had hammered out a new version with Shaun.

London theatres did not like the new version any more than they had the old but one day, having lunch with Philip Prowse, the designer at the Citizens Theatre, Glasgow, I threw my bag on to the restaurant floor beside the table and he noticed a script in it.

'What's that?' he asked, 'Got a job?'

'No', I said and swallowed, 'I want to direct it.'

'Why haven't you brought it to us?' he asked.

'Because, Philip, you almost always do classical plays. I am only a beginner and it is not your sort of thing.'

'What's it about?' he said.

'It's about angry boys, standing in pools of piss, swearing.'

His slim hand flew up to his shirt collar. 'But, Di', he said, 'it sounds right up my street.'

We laughed and a week later, stuck for something to put into the programme between the panto and the three classical plays of the spring season – a usually dead part of the year when audiences were low after Christmas, and they thought they might as well risk it – the Citizens programmed *Desperado Corner*. They asked me in return to be in the first part of the season as an actress and I duly gave the Glasgow audience the pleasure of my peasant wife in Brecht's *Caucasian Chalk Circle* and Marie Antoinette in a new David MacDonald play where, dressed in a wig twelve inches high and a gown of silver-encrusted brocade, I arrived on stage from the back of a truck.

I was a member of the acting company on the Saturday night and a director of a new play the following Monday. By Monday evening, I knew I had found my life's work. Then I started careering.

18

THE PLAYS AND POETRY OF A GERMAN AND A SPANIARD

Two writers have dominated my life – one Spanish and one German.

I knew, as soon as I was capable of knowing anything, that there were people called Germans who had bombed my parents out of house and home, who had trapped my mother and new-born brother in a cellar under the rubble until an air-raid warden had carried the baby off to an unknown shelter and my mother had sought him desperately for two days. Whenever thunderstorms came in my childhood I saw my mother, shaking with anxiety, sheltering under the stairs, her eyes covered, reminded of the bombing. In time, I heard on the morning wireless that the brave British and Americans were staging an airlift to Berlin where the wicked Russians had blocked the overland routes to the western half of the city – and finally on a grainy black and white TV set I saw not only the Queen's Coronation but footage of a camp called Belsen with a man called Dimbleby saying that words defied description of the suffering, the starvation and the savagery those Germans had inflicted there. 'I have lived through two wars', my grandmother said grimly, 'and Germans have ruined my life.'

I did not know then of a German called Brecht.

I did not know there were Germans who had wanted before the war all that I was gaining after it – orange juice for their children, housing they could afford, jobs. That there were Germans who had predicted just that savagery and just those word-defying camps. What I knew was my childhood round, its prejudices and its joys – chief among which was my Saturday tap-dancing class at Brenda Holland's Dancing School, where on the wooden floorboards of the local Church hall with an upright piano in the corner, I learnt the time-steps and the cramp-rolls I can still do to this day. Tap-dancing was the first real passion of my life – and even as I type in a Californian study, over fifty years later, I can feel the thrill of the syncopated rhythms tapping through my feet and above all the pre-war tunes that the elderly gentleman pianist knew best. And it was this – the sound of an old piano, the cadences of the 1930s – that filled me with a shock of recognition and sheer love when I first heard Lotte Lenya's voice singing from a record and heard the name of a German poet, Bertolt Brecht:

> In the dark times
> Will there be singing?
> Yes, there will also be singing
> About the dark times.

But this did not happen until I went to university. One night in my nineteenth year when I had been an undergraduate for only a few weeks, I was walking with a friend on the seafront in Brighton, bent against a chill wind, the sea crashing on the shingle beach below us, when he paused to introduce me to an acquaintance passing in the opposite direction. I stopped, turned and instantly fell in love. And here the complexities of class and politics took another turn. My young beloved was part Egyptian Jew, part English upper class, educated at Eton College, a socialist and as much in flight from his background as I was from mine. He taught me many things – about Brecht, amber worry beads, Egyptian fellaheen, old Cretan love songs and Gauloise cigarettes.

But most importantly, one night when I scarcely knew him he took me to see in a distant lecture theatre at Sussex University, a film called *To Die in Madrid*. There I saw the story of the fight for the Spanish Republic, with the voices of John Gielgud and Irene Worth and grainy footage from the Civil War, with a glimpse of the Spanish poet Federico Garcia Lorca laughing by a fountain. 'Green, green how I love you green,' Worth's beautiful voice intoned. That night my politics were decided for good. I would always be on the side of the raggedy brigades of workers, day labourers and subsistence farmers who had vowed to die on their feet rather than live on their knees. And I saw the German communist Thalmann Brigade, the earliest of the volunteers for the International Brigades, marching to the Battle of Madrid – and I decided then that German or Spanish, Brummagem or old Etonian, what mattered was whose side you were on.

Later, out of university, working in Compendium Bookshop in Camden Town, I struck up a conversation with a customer. He told me he and a group of friends were about to go to Morocco in a camper van to buy rugs and pottery to sell later in the year at Portobello market. I told him I had studied anthropology and was interested in all things Arabic. I had separated from the man with the amber worry beads and was in the worst throes of jealousy, scarcely able to eat or sleep. I seized at a chance to get away. A week later with a week's wages in my pocket I set off with the stranger and his friends for Tangiers. Like Blanche Dubois, I have always relied on the kindness of strangers.

Morocco in those days was like another world. Hippies had begun visiting in the 1960s and by the time we got to the port of Ceuta at the tip of Spain, the frontier police were turning away western visitors with long hair and hippie clothes. We were refused entry. We found a cheap rooming house in the back streets and I cut all the men's hair with my nail scissors, took off my long dress, put on a tight fitting skirt and jacket, put my hair up in a French pleat and walked through the frontier on foot to meet them the other side. We were a strange mixture typical of that 1960s world – Gavin, my bookshop customer, a hippy with entrepreneurial ambitions and a bit of family money; his business partner, a savvy young Cockney with his wife and young baby (called Anna Morning Star); a heroin-addict friend of theirs trying to force himself into recovery; a schoolmate of Gavin's just out of a Canadian prison (for dope-dealing); and a pretty redhead brought along for her decorative qualities and, I suspected, easy morals. I have never met anyone with so limited a vocabulary as this girl: she used two adjectives – yin and yang – and infuriated us all after a few days. 'Oh this weather,' she would sigh, 'so ...', and we would all know one or other of the epithets was about to come, '... yang.'

Arriving through Tangiers, a town I came to love and first saw now in the golden sun of an afternoon in April, we did not stop but drove straight through the hills towards a mountain village which Gavin had heard of in the Rif mountains called Chefchaouen. Night was falling when we stopped to swap over drivers. I stepped out and, walking away from my companions, saw shadowy hills. Under foot grew wild mint and the scent of it filled the warm air. All was silent in the hills except for a distant sound of running water. I was enchanted. And Morocco has never lost its enchantment for me, for in it I found as if in pentamento, the Spain of Lorca. Chefchaouen was a white Berber village built on four hills with a newer Spanish part in a valley and the old walled town tumbling around steep cobbled paths above. We found cheap muleteers lodgings in the back of the square up an alleyway. The windows had no glass, just wooden shutters and it was cold. In the dawn I was awoken by my first bout of food poisoning – there were many to come – and I found the lavatory – a freezing hole in the ground – at the end of a corridor. As I vomited and groaned, a thin light came through a chink in the shutters and I heard for the first time the muezzin calling from the mosque – Allah is great – I took deep breaths and despite my discomfort and the sinister smells, thought – this is the life for me.

Within days, the men had negotiated the rental of a four-storied white house at the edge of the village. We all went to dinner with the landlord to celebrate, spoke broken Spanish, and ate with our fingers from one central dish. On the roof, a doorless room with a tap became our kitchen once we had bought two charcoal burners and some plates and dishes. I went into the souk and bought a blanket, some leather slippers and a scarf. The blanket, thick and coloured at one end, turned out to be somewhat thinner and less coloured at the other – the end the shopkeeper did not unroll towards me over his stall, but cheated or not I still liked it and made a simple bed on the floor of a downstairs room where the stream outside gave me the sound I already loved from my first night. Apart from a rat appearing out of the hole in the ground of our basement lavatory the first time I visited it, I soon became adept at this new life – shopping in the produce market in the square, squatting, bellows in hand, over the braziers and even venturing with a tray of food to the local oven where along with the bread or *hubz* (my first Arabic word) all the villagers took food for baking.

It was always tiresome to go anywhere alone. You were surrounded by children chattering, pulling at your clothes and begging for money and attention. The older men often followed you too, making ribald gestures or simply staring. I soon covered my hair and wore loose-fitting dresses with long sleeves but it made no difference. I was a foreigner and a female one. As for the women: mountain women or *jblya* went unveiled; those in the town were more likely to be wrapped in a *chador* – a white cotton cloth swept around the body, head and face – and they slipped silently past me in the alleyways and through wooden gates in the walls of their houses or made their way with their donkeys back to their hamlets at the end of market days.

Soon young Arab men visited the house, bringing with them drums and *kif* (powdered hashish) which we smoked in tiny pipes or sipses. We drank endless glasses of sweet mint tea and the men in the party arranged visits to the hashish fields of Ketama and set up contacts in Marrakesh, and then suddenly early one morning they were gone, leaving me and the redhead behind to look after the house on our own. I knew why they had not taken me with them – tired of the other girl and her vacuous conversation, they had hesitated to leave her alone. Since I had turned out to be a reluctant sexual partner to any of the available males, efficient at housekeeping and happy to stay in Chefchaouen, they left me too.

We had visitors – a travel writer I met in the square with a motor caravan, a typewriter and an African boy from Mali. Then one day on our way to the post office in the Spanish sector, we saw a young man in jeans and boots leading a horse. He stopped and spoke to me in French, asking where he could stay and later came to the house for dinner and to sleep in one of the many empty rooms. Some of the drumming *kif* smokers turned up too and as we sat on the roof in a circle after dinner and as the pipes went around he turned to me and said, 'These people are no good. This is not the real Morocco.'

'Where is the real Morocco then?' I asked.

'Out there,' he said, with a gesture towards the mountain, 'where I am going.'

Jean Louis had travelled with his horse from the Algerian border and had been living for some months in a one-roomed shack some miles from Chefchaouen. He had come down to pick up post, and buy food and charcoal. Next morning, he was ready to leave by the time I got up and went to the door to say goodbye. His horse was saddled and laden and he held him by the bridle. I said, mustering my best schoolgirl French, 'Bon voyage,' and he walked back towards me and said, 'Viens avec moi.' I turned, went back to my room, rolled my things into the blanket and went with him.

I now began to live life in the mountains of the Rif with no running water or sanitation, in one room with an unglazed window overlooking the valley. We slept on a pile of sheepskins under woollen blankets and cooked over a brazier in the small fenced paddock beside the house. I loved everything – the misty valley in the mornings, the hillside, the nights full of stars when we would light a fire and slowly in the darkness we could make out other fires burning on the opposite hillside. In the morning, a boy of about ten herding goats would play a little wooden pipe sitting cross-legged on a rock above the house and I would walk to a spring where I collected water from a spout made from a folded leaf tucked under a rock. Life was like those little coloured Bible pictures they gave out at Sunday school.

There was a concrete water tank below the spring which was used for irrigation and sometimes I would bathe in it, washing and rinsing myself first from a bucket. I had one novel and an exercise book in which I wrote a diary. Later we made a journey through the Rif mountains to the Mediterranean at Oued Laou. We walked beside the horse most of the day along winding paths or dirt roads overhung with ripe mulberries with wild oleanders in the ravines below. Occasionally, we would pass a café with a dirt floor, some mint tea and a few provisions on the shelves – vegetables, washing powder, tinned sardines, sugar. We would buy some onions and tomatoes from the shopkeeper, he would measure a cup of olive oil and then cook it up into a delicious mess for us, finally breaking into it two eggs. This we would eat with fresh baked flat bread, with all the customers silently watching my every move, and then when the café emptied, we would hand the owner a few dirhams for the privilege, push a table against the door, spread out our blankets and sleep on the floor. In the morning there would be coffee with sweetened tinned milk and we would go on our way again.

We passed remote mountain villages where the Berber women went unveiled with woven shawls – *mendils* – wrapped around the waist like skirts and leather gaiters on their legs. The children ran around us, bare feet and tangled hair with big dark eyes ringed by kohl and we were asked for medicine – once for a donkey with a great saddle sore. I gave the owner a half-used tin of antiseptic cream, but soon had given away all our aspirin and antibiotics. The women were always busy – bent over the earth, sweeping their rough courtyards, catching screaming toddlers up in their arms. The men sat against the walls of their houses talking or stretched out in the shade of trees in the heat of the day to sleep. They only ever wanted one thing: a way to get to Europe to earn money. Again and again they asked us to invite them to our country to work – the only route to a passport and escape.

The villages were beautiful with streams gushing down from the mountains, the square flat-roofed houses built into the hillsides and with fig trees overhanging the doorways. But below the surface was dire poverty and illness. Tuberculosis was rampant and child after child had livid eye infections and mouth sores. I saw a family in a village by the sea, children, mother and grandmother all stricken with measles and its ensuing complications, gummy-eyed and feverish lying in a dark fetid room. There was a clinic some miles away, manned by a young English doctor from Notting Hill and always overflowing with patients and under-stocked with medicines, but you had to get there first. It was while living in a cave on the shore beyond Oued Laou that I had my first experience of the excruciating pain of migraine with absolutely no analgesics to help me. I might have been returned for a day to the Middle Ages. I lay almost unable to move, sure I was dying, wracked by vomiting for over twelve hours when slowly the pain began to lift and I walked into the sea where, the warm waves breaking over me, I experienced an unforgettable ecstasy: the cessation of agony. No pain in my life has ever equalled a severe migraine. It has taught me a grudging understanding of the addict for when in the throes of it, there is nothing I would not do, nothing I would not beg, borrow or steal to stop the pain. The only other agony I had experienced equal to it was the mental anguish of jealousy. And now I was learning that there is no drug for jealousy but time.

I suppose I went, to quote the British in India, native. The mountain women henna'd their hands – in intricate patterns when they were to be married. I too had my hands henna'd and put kohl powder in my eyes with a carved stick. I covered my hair with a woven red and green scarf but that did not prevent lice. When I finally got to Spain on my way home, I stood under a boiling hot shower for half an hour and tooth-combed them all out onto the marble tiles on the floor in a shower of dark brown specks. I did not understand I should oil my hair as the Moroccan women did which would have helped prevent them.

I only got to know one woman at all well. She lived in a room above the mule stable at the side of the village square. This was a beautiful crumbling building with balconies running in two storeys above a central dirt courtyard open to the sky – a vast riad of the kind that sells now for thousands in the old parts of Fez and Marrakesh. In ground-floor alcoves over little fires worked all kinds of metal craftsmen, and at the end a blacksmith. It was, on every market day, jostling with mules and men and packages and panniers and shouting. Jean-Louis took his horse there one morning to be shod and the woman leaning over the balcony, her long black hair hanging loose, gestured to me to come up and showed me into the room where she plied her trade. It was a whore's room from a nineteenth-century French novel with faded pictures on the wall above a sagging metal bed, a hanging light, and a sweet smell. We struck up an odd kind of friendship and I got to recognize her by her eyes when she walked through the village in a *chador*.

One day she showed me a Moroccan dance. She stretched her hands to the side of her head, clapped the heels of her palms together and stamped her bare feet. I saw in that gesture, the sordo of flamenco and suddenly realized that Southern Spain was not Spanish at all but Moorish – those white villages of the Alpujarras were Berber with a pot of white paint thrown over them, and the gesture of the hand over the mouth when Spanish peasant women addressed strangers was a reflex of the veil. I was seeing what Spain had been in the early years of the century.

Late one market day, we began the journey home in the cool of the afternoon with our shopping – little paper packages of rice, beans, soap and beignets or unsweetened doughnuts fried in the souk and threaded onto a circle of grass. On the track up to our cottage we were halted by a group of dogs barking and snarling at our heels, and an old farmer in a djelaba and slippers came out of his house to control them – shouting, kicking and beating them with a stick. He addressed us in Spanish and I emerged from Jean-Louis' shadow and started to talk – a mangled mixture of gesture and broken Spanish, playing nervously with the edge of my scarf over my mouth. His farm, the man explained proudly, was purchased from the money he had earned 'over the sea'. He gestured admiringly at the terrain – green terraces spread across the hillside. He was relatively wealthy – a small landowner. I recognized in his torrent of speech two words – *la guerra* and Badajoz. He made a gesture with his hands and made the sound of gunfire with a laugh. Then asking us to wait he dragged the dogs back on their chains, fastened them horribly short, went into the house and came out with a white circle of goat's cheese wrapped in plaited straw as a gift. I could look only at the dogs cowed and whimpering, the chains pulling cruelly on their necks. With smiles and waves and gestures of hand to heart, he bid us goodbye and we walked on, following a water course around the hillside. The air was just beginning to cool: it would soon be night. And I thought of the old farmer and the young desperate men in the villages and other men years before in Spain, desperate too, who had tried to change their poverty-stricken lives.

I knew at once the old farmer had been a mercenary and I had heard of Badajoz – anyone with any knowledge of the Spanish Civil War had. In the Civil War, Badajoz had been taken after a bloody battle by Franco's Moorish mercenaries who had then sacked the town and killed thousands of prisoners and civilians, culminating in an infamous round of executions in the bull ring. The massacre in Badajoz was not a unique case in the march of Yagüe's column from Seville, when over six thousand people were killed in the eastern part of the province of Badajoz. Most of the victims were journeymen and farmers.

I walked on, the water gurgling at my feet, a terrible rage of conflicting sympathies in my heart and tried to remember a poem which began, 'At five in the afternoon …'. Slowly it came back to me; it was Lorca's epitaph to the bullfighter – 'Llanto por Ignacio Sánchez Mejías' – and could serve as an epitaph to all who had died in that most bitter of wars including the poet himself.

> At precisely five in the afternoon
> A boy brought the white sheet.
> At five in the afternoon
> A basket of lime stood ready.
> The rest was death, and only death.[1]

In that moment was born me a determination to stage the plays of Brecht and Lorca and to live according to the Spanish poet's credo – 'I will always,' he said, 'be on the side of those who have nothing.'

And thus I started not only to love the sound of Lenya's voice, but also the meaning of Brecht's words and above all the excitement – the release even – of his kind of theatre. He loved, as I did, the excitement of the fairground, the boxing ring, the wooden planks and the standing crowds, the hurdy-gurdy and the song sung for its meaning not the voice beautiful. His theatre with its insistence on obvious story-telling, scene titles and the ever-present sister art – music – seemed fresh even in the early 1960s.

It was at Sussex that I first acted in Brecht: I was the coolie in *The Exception and the Rule* – one of the lesser-known didactic or teaching plays. I had absolutely no notion of Brechtian theories of acting and barely understood 'verfremdung' or – and what a poor translation it is – alienation technique. What I vaguely understood was that the audience should realize I was an actor playing a role and thus, between my bits of dialogue, I would self-consciously stand as myself and not as a coolie. What our little student audience made of all this, I do not know but Buzz Goodbody, a fellow student, already on the way to the Royal Shakespeare Company and her short but brilliant career, suggested the coolie should carry a portable TV and quite mystified me.

I saw her next piece of work in Trafalgar Square shortly afterwards when with a feminist street-theatre company, one of the actresses burnt a bra. I knew then that Buzz understood the new struggle in gender politics as I did not, but I was filled with a yearning to learn more. She wrote to me later about auditioning for the Royal Shakespeare Company but before anything came of it she had committed suicide. Her fate burned through my mind in all my subsequent dealings with that company and made me more tough and uncompromising than I would have otherwise been. Her production of *Hamlet*, which used a small company, Ben Kingsley in the lead, was a stripped down version full of invention with a paper crown as one of the props. It was not the success of this that weighed with Buzz but her subsequent failure on the main stage.

When it came to my failure on the same main stage, I came near to experiencing the same order of despair but I soon had a secret bulwark against all the disdain and criticism: I was pregnant – a production as I told the *Guardian* critic Michael Billington in a corridor of the Barbican, 'you are not going to review'. I had unknowingly hit upon the gulf that separates men from women – they are creative but we hold the trump card, we are also recreative and after all, another human life is the real thing: the rest is a mere counterfeit.

At the Citizens Theatre, Glasgow I had my chance to play Joan Dark in Brecht's *St Joan of the Stockyards*. I took the part seriously. I was after all working on what was referred to as the Red Clyde – where miners and shipbuilders had learned to fight hard for their rights. Glasgow was still poverty stricken with teeming tenements and slums that were referred to as the worst in Europe. I was busy politically selling a Trotskyist newspaper in pubs and trying to interest the unemployed youth in becoming politically active – although by this time heroin was beginning to make inroads on the new high-rise estates and the old streets. The old Communist Party was still going strong and I met some dedicated people – ex-miners who had gone to night school and got degrees and old men wonderfully cogent about the world situation – and couldn't understand why the Left was so split. Yet.

Ironically, for by this time I was obsessed with motherhood, the production which really taught me about Brecht was *The Mother* which I first directed at the Contact Theatre in Manchester during the miners' strike and later at the National Theatre in the Cottesloe. The miners struck under Thatcher and picketed the power stations where violence erupted as scab labour was bussed in and the police went at the crowds with tear gas and horses. The miners' wives fought at the beginning on the domestic front, manning centres where food was donated and providing meals for the strikers' families but soon began to join their husbands more directly in the struggle. Their anthem was, 'Whose side are you on?'

It was the Brecht translator and expert John Willett who properly introduced me to the plays of Brecht and he who suggested I direct *The Mother* – a play I found rather dry and didactic on paper but (as is the case with so many of the plays) fascinating, funny and utterly theatrical on stage. It is about a mother uninterested in politics who discovers during a strike that to stay human, she has to decide whose side she is on. It could not have been more apt and in my production in Manchester I linked it directly with the events unfolding on the streets outside – running news clips of the miners' strike on television screens through the scene changes and echoing these modern images in the scenes. Here too I discovered the brilliance of Hans Eisler, Brecht's composer – to my mind far greater than Kurt Weill whose work is better known.

My fascination with Brecht grew ever stronger when, during rehearsals of Lorca's *Yerma* at the National Theatre, I married Dominic Muldowney who worked with Willett on a BBC production of Brecht's first play *Baal* with David Bowie in the lead. Bowie's rendition of the 'Ballad of Marie A' is the finest singing of a Brecht song I have ever heard. Later Dominic recorded two albums of Brecht's songs in English with the Australian singer Robyn Archer and a memorable track on 'Reach for the Stars' where Sting sang 'Mack the Knife' and I persuaded them to add the spoken introduction: 'Soho: the thieves are thieving, the whores are whoring and a street-singer sings ...'.

I was always interested in Brecht's work with Caspar Neher, his designer, and loved anecdotes about Brecht's insistence on the actors using the perfectly correct worn prop; how they tried chair after chair until they got the right one which would allow an actor to slide comically from chair to table in one move; how the soldiers in *Mother Courage* slowly and methodically prepared the gun before shooting down the dumb daughter. I noted with delight how the half-curtain could work and loved a production style which never let us forget we were in the theatre. But most of all, I looked always for the notion of 'Spass' in Brecht's work – fun. You can hear something of it in the liveliness of the recording of *Mahagonny* by the Berliner Ensemble. As for acting, I never found so-called Brechtian style a problem with modern actors and discovered that the responsibility for the actors' 'gestus' – an acting term which suggests a combination of physical gesture and character attitude – really lay with the director patiently paring away at truthfully observed character and finding a style that renders the story-telling theatrical, punchy and unsentimental. With my production of *The Mother* came praise for the staging but criticism for the modern parallels I drew – an inevitable tendency of all English criticism of Brecht whose political outlook most of the critics would rather were consigned to the history books. None of that political stuff, they always claim, is relevant today.

The same happened years later when I directed *Fear and Misery of the Third Reich* and drew parallels between the peat bog soldiers of the camps and the untried prisoners of Guantanamo Bay and those delivered to the hands of foreign state torturers (including the Moroccan government) by rendition, so that Britain and the USA could maintain their hypocrisy – growing every day to new heights – that they play no part in torture. This I called *Fear and Misery of the New Right* and in it Harold Pinter allowed me to use part of his Nobel acceptance speech where, like a figure from Beckett huddled in a wheelchair, he had denounced US imperialism.

Later I was to stage *The Resistible Rise of Arturo Ui* at the Olivier Theatre with Antony Sher in the role of the gangster Ui, modelled on Hitler. Here, I have to concede, is a play that sits uneasily in the modern theatre when all we know of the Holocaust makes us less able to appreciate the satire of Hitler as a gangster-buffoon. Until that point in history no gangster or his compliant henchmen, not even in Brecht's worst imaginings in the first years of his exile in Finland, had had the technology of the gas chambers at his command.

I devised a tribute to Brecht at the Royal National Theatre on the centenary of his birth, as I did to Lorca fifty years to the day after his murder at Fascist hands in the first days of the Spanish Civil War. As much as I have loved the plays of both writers – I have directed *Yerma* and *The House of Bernarda Alba* and many of Brecht's plays – what I really started to appreciate is the stature of Brecht too as a poet. I have often heard Brecht described as an unashamed apologist of Stalin, but in his poetry you find all the anguish of one who has survived one hideous struggle only to find another is to be fought, and this with those whom he had thought of as comrades:

> the travails of the mountains lie behind us
> Before us lie the travails of the plains.

A conversation in 1998 with Brecht's assistant Carl Weber[2] about the anguish in Brecht's company when the uprising of 17 June 1956 was raging outside, and the endless debate about what the company should do, convinced me that it was never easy for Brecht to accept Stalinism. Brecht came to the defence of the young writer Martin Pohl, for whom he wrote an affidavit, although Pohl was later given four years in prison. And he was

> in constant dispute with the organs of the state, especially about cultural policy. He was an irritation to them, as well as being wanted as a 'cultural advertisement' for the new state. He may have taken care not to give the capitalist west the comfort of openly disagreeing with the Party line, but there are enough private remarks and coded critiques in the works to show his real feelings.[3]

On the other hand he couldn't relinquish his long-term faith in and commitment to the Communist Party and the Soviet Union – a faith that had moulded him intellectually. In his poem 'Die Losung' or 'The Solution' he could not be more clear in his frustration at the government of the GDR when, after the uprising, they distributed leaflets in the Stalinallee saying that the people had forfeited the confidence of the government:

> Would it not be easier
> In that case for the government
> To dissolve the people
> And elect another?

Brecht died early of heart disease and it may be sentimental but I often think that post-war life in East Germany, even with all his international theatrical triumphs, worked in the secret recesses of Brecht's heart and finally broke it.

It was the fate of both Lorca and Brecht to be forged as men and artists in the furnace of inter-war twentieth-century politics – that epoch, as Lenin described it, of wars and revolutions. Both hated Fascism – Lorca trusted a Fascist family with his life and they handed him over to one of their officer friends whose thugs killed him, slung him into an unmarked grave and denied for years the responsibility for doing so. Brecht embraced the only really serious political opposition to Fascism and he saw the Soviet Union triumph but pay with the price of twenty million dead. His own illegitimate son, born when he was a young man singing to his guitar in local cafes, died with the German Sixth Army at the Russian front. Contradictions ran through his whole life. His feelings and mine are best expressed in his poem 'Changing the Wheel':

> I sit by the road as my driver
> Changes the wheel.
> I do not like where I have come from. I
> Do not like where I am going. Why
> Do I watch him change the wheel
> With impatience?

19

THINGS FRENCH

I remember nothing of the journey there. I only remember emerging from the Metro into the Boulevard St Michel: the evening sun, plane trees, pavement cafés, wine glasses, brown feet in canvas espadrilles, copper bracelets on thin arms, the sound of drumming drifting through the warm air, water gushing from the great stone fountain of Saint Michael plunging a spear through the cringing devil. It seemed in that golden moment of my eighteenth year, as if not only Satan but all the ugliness in my life had been vanquished. Paris. Paris, mon amour.

That first time, when meals on a *menu fixe* could be had for four francs and my young companion and I lived by a book called *Europe on Five Dollars a Day*, we dawdled through France, hitch-hiking vaguely south coming upon villages and towns by the whim of the drivers who picked us up. We bought tomatoes and a baguette for picnic lunches and spent the nights in cheap rooms over cheap restaurants. Rooms were simple and spare with enormous old bedsteads, faded photographs, and enamel bidets on stands with an accompanying jug of water and a slop bucket. We ate eggs with mayonnaise, melons, strawberry tarts with Chantilly cream, cassoulets and coq au vin and in the mornings, great steaming bowls of café au lait with croissants and thick fruit-filled home-made jams. We walked down roads lined with shimmering poplars and into markets over stone bridges and tumbling rivers. Apple orchards gave way to vineyards and vineyards to fields of sunflowers and then to the Mediterranean sea: 'mon enfant, ma soeur, songe a la douceur'.[1]

Years later, my husband earned some money writing the music for a movie. We decided to travel around the world and for a taste of the travelling life, we drove to Spain and Morocco, returning through Normandy. After only a few weeks, we had realized that my husband was tired of moving on and living out of suitcases and, crucially, could not write any music. We looked at an old farmhouse on a hill, agreed that what both of us had always dreamed of was to live in France and went to the lawyer's office in Bacqueville en Caux and made enquiries. The farmhouse was named le Bout du Haut – Highfield – I realized joyously. We bought it and in it I tried to recreate the felicities of my godparents' house of that name. We were about twenty-five miles from the port of Dieppe, seven hours journey by boat and car from London and in a different world.

We moved in a few weeks later with a mattress, an electric cooker, an old ping-pong table and some garden chairs the former owner had left behind. It was autumn by now and the apple trees were laden with fruit. Our garden had been hacked out of the adjoining farmland and orchard. The local grocer delivered an oak cask, the plumber some empty bottles, and one afternoon the portable press trundled down the long lane to the house and in an hour the apples piled against the tree trunks had been squeezed into juice, decanted into the cask and laid in the cellar to foment into cider. We stacked piles of apple wood and oak in the woodshed and bought firedogs for the great brick kitchen fireplace, as tall as a man and stretching nearly the width of the wall. Slowly, the house grew around us. We took out all the hideous modernizations, the pink bathroom, the brown tiled scullery, the bedroom wallpaper. Two young scene painters, the Kalitowski brothers, came from London and painted the walls – ochre fading to yellow on the staircase and miles of French grey in the downstairs rooms. I bought muslin and hung long curtains lying in folds on the wooden floors as Karen Blixen had done in Africa. Dominic moved his workroom into the attic which had a great wood-beamed roof hammered in with oak pegs by Dieppe boat builders. From the outside the house was plain, austere even with five symmetrical upstairs windows, an attic dormer and shallow steps to the double front door, but it faced south and was filled with light and over the outside walls grew a massive Virginia creeper. Its rooms were all high ceilinged and large. A tiled entrance hall from which rose a curving wide staircase gave way to four downstairs rooms and two sculleries. Upstairs from a wide landing, you could walk from one bedroom to another by connecting doors. There was one bathroom. We never got around to putting in others. We couldn't decide which of the lovely symmetrical rooms to spoil.

We never got around to lots of things. Life and work took us back and forth to London, and we would sink back into the house the way it was, not wanting to spoil the days with changes and hammering. So the back door let in drafts and the upstairs windows never got shuttered and the wall down to the cellar remained damp. We were happy though, dressed

against the cold during the winter days and in front of a blazing log fire at
night, reading plays, planning projects, music pouring out of the attic and
productions pencilled into next year's diary. In the summer came long
lovely days where we went to the sea at Veules les Roses, walked far away
down the beach, lit a fire and cooked sausages and hamburgers in a cast
iron frying pan. We laughed with our friends and ate, wet haired and salty
mouthed from swimming, and watched the waves pounding the pebbled
shore. Dominic mowed in the grass that bordered the house the name of
our new daughter, adopted from across the ocean in El Salvador. 'We are
happy', we said to each other, 'We are the luckiest people in the world.'

Then our world fell apart. Sunt lacrimae rerum. There are things of
tears and nothing more bleak than the dark-eyed child, Vita, named for
life itself, diagnosed as brain damaged half a year later, all our hopes
dashed and a great tsunami of pity and helplessness swamping every
waking hour. I struggled to work, to stage at Stratford a play I had
contracted to do before my daughter's fate had become the only thing
that mattered, where the line 'a star danced and under that was I born'
made me want to cry out.

I fled back to the house and its echoing barely filled rooms, hearing
a baby who was no longer mine crying distantly and no way to find
her. Reviews lamented that I seemed to have lost my touch, that one
of Shakespeare's most sparkling comedies seemed misjudged and lack-
lustre in my hands. I stopped working. I threw next year's diary with its
dates of future productions into the wastepaper bin. No longer a director,
no longer a mother, I did not know who I was.

The minutiae of French domestic life filled my day. I became Madame
Muldowney. I spoke French without noticing which language I spoke. I
marketed every morning, basket in hand, only for the meals of that day –
placing slim brown paper packages of the day's ingredients on the kitchen
table and bread fresh from the boulangerie every morning and evening.
I cooked, I sewed, I painted, I upholstered old armchairs and decorated
screens. I bottled apricots in gin and cherries in brandy. I walked – across
the fields, along the beaches, through the woods. Sometimes the phone
rang and a familiar voice from one of the London theatre companies
would politely ask to speak to my husband. All that life – the stage doors,
the offices, the casting meetings, the drives to Stratford, the rehearsal
rooms, the company of actors, the slog, the laughter, the excitement, the
exhaustion: all was now as if lost.

And then by a miracle, I gave birth to a child I had been told I could
never have and in the snows of the Easter of 1989, I took her to France
and laid her in the nursery with its grey striped walls and cherry red

curtains and the angelus ringing out over the fields at seven in the morning and seven in the evening, measuring out her first spring days. Life staggered to its feet again. I loved the new child but as if in a dream, all tinged with unreality, and a self – stout and plain in the mirror – barely recognizable from only two years before. My husband – musical director at the National Theatre – travelled to London and technical rehearsals and first nights, and brought me occasional news of that strange land from which I now felt entirely exiled.

How had it happened that the world I had longed for, worked for, striven for, the world that had been my alpha and omega had slipped from my grasp like a stone into a stream? I missed it with a deep, hidden guilty longing for I had my precious child and should have been happy, for she walked and talked and toddled off into the garden and learned the French for cow and hide and seek and called me maman. And all the time, Time gnawed at me – the notion that it was passing and I was somehow going to waste. I would look at the palms of my hands and see nothing but emptiness and the unfathomable lines that were supposed to tell my future. Alone at night, with my husband at work in London and the child asleep upstairs, I would pace the house and garden, venturing down the long track from the house to the road, looking southwards and dream of walking on and on into the night. Back in the house smelling of wood smoke and beeswax, I would listen to the wind in the trees and the steady rhythm of my daughter's breath as she lay sleeping and wonder why it was not enough. I counted the years since I had entered a rehearsal room – three already – and all that I had achieved seemed a dream.

Then one day, unpacking cartons of books that had been sent from England, I came across a copy of Harold Pinter's screenplay of *Remembrance of Things Past* by Marcel Proust. I took one look at the opening page, settled down among the packing cases and read it without interruption. Where was the child? Gone, I think, with her father to collect milk in her special wooden-handled tin canister from the neighbouring farm.

As I looked out of the window of that French house, I realized that beyond the apple trees in the orchard lay a lane bordered in spring with white hawthorn. Across the endless plain between Longueville and Luneray, you could see the church spires dancing on the horizon. On the door of my house was a bell set upon a curve of metal which rang each time someone entered. I had come without quite knowing it to the country of Proust. I had started to read Proust several times as a young woman but I never got past the first few pages. I always thought as I put the first volume back in the shelves, 'There will be time'. But as we know and even more vividly once we have read Proust, time is elusive, life passes – as Beckett said, 'It would have passed anyway'.

I always thought a day would come when life would deal me a hard blow – a prolonged stay in hospital or enforced bed-rest during pregnancy – one day, in fact, the sheer weight of the tedium of my own miserable life would force me to embrace Proust's seemingly endless perorations and I would at last be let in on the secret of the few who actually enjoyed *À La Recherche du Temps Perdu*. How, as a young woman, in love with all things French, that little word 'perdu' already had the power to fascinate me. In my second language which I had just been beginning to conquer, as my French boyfriend joked, on the pillow – 'sur l'oreiller' – 'perdu' could mean lost or wasted but did not mean past. Even he, the other head upon my Parisian pillow, admitted he had not read Proust. 'Un jour,' he said, 'un jour il y'aura le temps.'

There never was time. The affair ended. I left Paris. The years had passed. I had become an actress. I had played Odette in a stage version of Proust's work by Robert David Macdonald but had only dipped haphazardly into the first volume, scanning it for character clues. Now, the time – the time of tedium and the time of wasting time – had come.

I immediately began the novels – there are three thick volumes in a translation by Scott-Montcrieff – even then not in a solid scholarly way – there was the child after all – but looking for sections that fascinated me in the screenplay and then becoming engrossed in some particular and reading on. And all the time I thought that it was the most terrible waste that Pinter's version had never been performed. I discovered that Joseph Losey had commissioned the screenplay and had struggled to raise the money to make the film. He and Harold Pinter had even met at the Ritz Hotel in Paris to celebrate finalizing the finances with the American producers, when they had been told, as they perused the menus and ordered champagne, that the whole deal had fallen through. The film never materialized. I knew too that the writing of it had taken up a whole year of Pinter's life.

Life continued its gentle pace in the French countryside, the seasons marked by the fruit from the garden tumbling about the kitchen table, last year's cider quenching the thirst of summer afternoons, beef en daube left overnight on the glowing cinders of winter fires, the wind howling in from the south east and bringing with it snow across the stubble fields. I read, I worried, I started tentatively to try to return to my old life. But doors that had stood wide open were closed, phone calls were left unreturned, ideas fell on deaf ears. In that bitter joke of the theatre – I couldn't get arrested. I started to direct again intermittently and at nothing like the old level. And slowly seven years passed.

Then in 1996, on a day of torrential rain which found me rehearsing Lorca's *The House of Bernarda Alba* at the Clywd Theatr in Wales, I was handed a piece of paper which said 'Please ring Peter Jones urgently'. I wondered all morning whether it was the Sloane Street department store chasing me for an unpaid account. Fortified only by the knowledge that Clwyd Theatr owed me the balance of my fee on the first night, I called back. It was in fact Peter James, English theatre director and principal of the London Academy of Dramatic Art. He asked me if there was an idea I would like to try out with a group of twenty-seven second year students. The work would last for four months – four afternoon sessions a week – investigating and devising a stage event which would be performed, if I felt the work had progressed enough, to an invited audience. We arranged to meet as soon as my Lorca production had opened.

By the time I drove to Peter James' office in the Cromwell Road a few weeks later, I had a couple of ideas worked out on a postcard. Then as I sat in his office waiting for the Head of Acting to join us, another idea fell into my head in incredible detail. I don't mean details of the actual version, but details of how to begin the work – the most you can ever wish for – and (thank God for the courage to follow an impulse) I told Peter I wanted to work on a new stage version of *Remembrance of Things Past*.

I went back to my house in London, got out a copy of the screenplay and promptly had a panic attack. In a diary entry for October of that year I wrote: 'Now I don't know what the fuck to do because it's twelve novels, a screenplay and lots of twenty-year-old students … can I translate any of it onto the stage?' What I did not write in my diary was that I was working in a cold and dirty church hall for not very much money and with comparatively few resources and I did not know what my life was coming to.

Four months later the students and I emerged with a performable evening in the theatre. I invited only a few colleagues, thinking almost to the last it would not work at all. Their response was overwhelmingly enthusiastic. They all urged me to go on with the project. I had managed to pry open a chink in a door.

But within only a few days, I had to fight a terrible inertia. From the camaraderie of the rehearsal room, I was catapulted into solitariness once more. What had seemed so concrete in the little theatre off the Cromwell Road seemed now like a chimera. The script looked like a child had pasted it together. My efforts seemed contemptible. I had not even enquired about the rights and, anyway, what theatre would undertake such a project? Only two theatres in the country had the resources – the Royal Shakespeare Company and the National Theatre – but would they have the appetite? Would I, could I ever work in either again? Any woman who has spent a few months at home with a child knows the unreality past achievements assume. Did I really do that? I would look at photographs of past productions and find it hard to believe they had ever happened. For some weeks the tatty script lay neglected on my desk, but then I gathered up the willpower – for it is nothing but willpower that gets you through these blacknesses – and finally opened it up and started working on another draft. It took two months.

Then came a nerve-wracking moment. I rang Harold Pinter and asked to see him. He made an appointment with me for Shrove Tuesday 1997 at 6pm. Such is the fate of a working mother that on the way there I worried not about the imminent meeting but that I had not had time to make my daughter pancakes for tea. I mounted the stairs to Harold's study and finally told him what I had done. I had been working all this time without his knowledge. I thought he might be furious and dismissive. He listened in silence and then poured two glasses of white wine and said, 'This sounds pretty interesting.' He told me that Trevor Nunn had asked to see a copy of the screenplay. Perhaps, he suggested, we should take the project to the National Theatre.

'Christ', I said, 'I hope no-one pinches my idea'. Harold suddenly looked very serious. 'Di, remember I own this screenplay and no-one else is going to do anything with it without my permission. After all, you've done all the work on it for months and you deserve the chance to do it. It is mine and', brushing back his black hair with his right hand – a characteristic gesture he often made when he had decided upon something, 'I'm not dead yet.' This was my first glimpse of Pinter loyalty. As I drove home, listening to BBC Radio 3 – Al Bowly singing at the Café de Paris – I felt absurdly happy.

I met Trevor Nunn the following week in his office on the fourth floor of the National Theatre's South Bank building with its enchanting view of the River Thames and organized a rehearsal room performance of the piece for him and a small invited audience – National Theatre staff, colleagues of Harold, Joseph Losey's widow. Pinter sat alone at the back of the room, intent and still, the rest of the audience in a single row of chairs in front. Even he, I thought with a jolt, looked nervous. Then I realized, this work had taken him a year to write and he had never seen it performed. I suddenly saw the whole thing as a kind of terrible audition. Instead of stepping forward and giving a little speech of welcome and explanation – most of the audience had no idea how the performance had come about – overcome by a paroxysm of nerves, I signalled to the stage manager to lower the lights and start. I then left the room and walked along the Embankment feeling sick and crushed, returning only in time for the last cue and Trevor Nunn to leap up, make a charming speech of thanks and Harold to cross to me and say 'It is good. We must go on with this', and most delightfully Pinteresque, 'you can certainly cut the mustard'.

A week later, the National Theatre commissioned the new version which Harold and I worked on together. I found myself in time taking my notebooks over to Ladbroke Grove where he worked in a cottage at the bottom of his garden and reading out ideas for scenes to him. It all seemed quite normal and we would read and discuss and alter and agree and disagree and come up with solutions and only from time to time would I remember that he was the author of all those plays I had revered as a young actress and wonder how I had the nerve. Once the script was finished, and we had agreed on it, I delivered it to Harold Pinter's typist so that it could be set out in the format he always used for his work. By next day, it was ready to be sent to the National Theatre. Then I had a phone call from Harold. He had discovered, he said, that Trevor Nunn was about to take the Concorde to New York. He was therefore having the script couriered to Heathrow airport so that Trevor would have it in his hands as he boarded the plane, 'Otherwise it will sit on his desk for weeks'. Here spoke the voice of experience.

Another year passed. We now settled back in London and my daughter put on a school uniform of corduroy breeches and a yellow skiing sweater and went to a school in Knightsbridge, where I envied her full school day and her walks to Hyde Park to play games. My days often weighed heavy on my hands.

Finally, in the summer of 1999, when I had almost entirely lost hope that something would come of it, it was tentatively agreed that the play would form part of the 2000 National Theatre season. I heard nothing officially. A friend from the administrative staff told me he had seen it written in pencil on a chart in an office on the fourth floor. At long last in the late autumn of 1999, it was set down in print on contracts and planning schedules.

Now all I had to do was direct it. And direct it I did, walking back into rehearsal Room 2 on the South Bank again for eight thrilling and exhausting weeks. Everything seemed to coalesce – the idea, the script, design, music, movement, my technical team and the company of actors.

Diary entries from the rehearsal period:

I have this amazing Pinter text to get spoken impeccably. I am just grateful Harold is away until the 30th which gives me seventeen days without his coming in and out. This really creative but seeming chaos will be over by then.

Next week we run the halves of the play and then by Friday, we will be running the play – you cannot imagine the staging that is in it – all done with twelve chairs and by the actors. There are two scenes which are especially striking – one at the seaside where we create a boardwalk, a beach, the sea, a restaurant, a hotel bedroom and a bandstand. The other scene is backstage at a theatre which simply teams with life – actresses resting, a ballet girl meeting her agent, dressers, stage hands, a man up a ladder, a fist fight between an aristocrat and a journalist – such fun.

The entire run is already sold out – was weeks ago. We appear in the list of the ten hottest tickets in London, 'before', it says in the paper, 'the play even opens.' Hardly any pressure at all.

I got to rehearsal a bit late, having taken D to the orthodontist, and was told Trevor wanted to see me urgently. I was shown straight into his office and he asked me to agree there and then that the Proust should transfer to the Olivier Theatre in February since it had sold out in the Cottesloe already. I reminded him that this project was the riskiest in the repertoire (the other plays being *Romeo and Juliet* and *Peer Gynt*) and such a transfer presumed a very great deal – press reaction, for instance. I said I would have to ask Harold what he thought. Trevor said he had already faxed him – he was in Italy – and got his approval. Typical tactics.

'When do you need to know?' I asked.

'At the end of the morning.'

When I got back to the rehearsal room, the company were finishing a movement class. Some of them are just beginning to waltz well. I decided not to say anything about a transfer until I felt better about it all.

Final run-through. Harold came yesterday. He said he would like to say a few words to the cast afterwards. They gathered around in a big half circle – their faces shiny and expectant – all actors are like hopeful children after a performance – and Harold said: 'I want to thank you all on behalf of Marcel Proust – I am a great friend of Marcel Proust'. He gave a little self-deprecating shrug of the shoulders – laughter – 'and I know he would want me to thank you for the great contribution you have brought to this. In my many long years in the theatre, I have rarely seen a production as thrilling and beautifully acted. You are a marvellous company.'

And then towards the end of its run in the Olivier theatre, I even got to act in it. One afternoon at about four o'clock, I got a phone call from a worried Company Manager. Diana Hardcastle, the actress playing the Duchesse de Guermantes, one of the most famous Proustian characters, had, while washing dishes, seriously cut a tendon in her hand on a piece of glass and could not appear that night. Because the play had transferred from the small Cottesloe Theatre where understudies were not employed, no actress was rehearsed and ready to play the part. I was asked if I could think of a solution. As I drove to the theatre, the paperback edition of the script open on the seat beside me, I realized that there was an actress to play the part: me.

Granted, I did not actually know the lines or the exact moves, but I had years before worked on the Olivier stage as an actress. I had adapted the play in two versions, directed it twice and I felt I could learn it in the few hours that remained between arriving at the theatre and performance. However, much of this time was taken up with finding me a corset and dresses I could squeeze into. The wardrobe mistress found pieces of Vanessa Redgrave's costumes from *The Cherry Orchard* in the maintenance wardrobe – combined them with things that fitted me from the Proust play and stitched me into them. The hairdresser found a false chignon that matched my hair colour and I practised in the tight high-heeled shoes, one size too small, walking across the raked stage in my long skirts to get my bearings. I sent out for green base make-up to disguise the scarlet nervous rash that had crept up my neck.

When I finally got to the wings to make my first entrance, with less than a minute to spare, the whole company looked at me in utter silence with sombre faces and staring eyes as if we were all at a funeral. I played the first scene to a Marcel – Sebastian Harcombe – visibly shaking with nerves, a script in my hand hidden under a gold lace shawl. But I didn't need to look at it. One of our first witty exchanges – one that I had written – got a laugh and I began to think it might just be alright.

I went over the lines for my second scene out loud with the assistant director Sarah Woolley as I changed into another swiftly assembled costume. Dressers lifted clothes on and off me without speaking as I repeated the text, assistant stage managers silently handed me props as I mouthed the lines to myself, fellow actors guided me to my entrance points. It all looked so very different from behind the scenes and in darkness.

Then I had the interval to learn the big scene in the second half of the play and then it was all over. When the curtain call came, we took three calls and the company moved in a semicircle behind me and I stood as if alone for a moment on the Olivier stage. 'I am back', I thought.

When I woke next morning, all the images of France flashed through my mind, the years I had thought my life in the theatre was over, the hours reading Proust, the long solitary walks pushing a pram along the hedge of white hawthorn. And I realized that in a small way I had, in an echo of Proust himself, recaptured what I had thought of as my own wasted time, in finally bringing to the stage a dramatic reconstruction of his. In learning how Proust was able to redeem Time, I had done so myself.

After breakfast, as we drew up in the car outside her school, my daughter asked what happened about the lady with the cut hand. 'I played her part', I said. 'Oh', she replied politely but by then she had already lost interest and was clambering out of the car door running to join her friends and live her new day.

Years later, on her way to being an undergraduate at Cambridge, she sat in Harold Pinter's cottage study and they talked of writing poetry and politics and gaunt with illness, he gave her some inscribed copies of his books. He was by then a Nobel Laureate. Looking from one beloved face to the other, I knew there had been no waste of Time there either.

NOTES

1 Space

1   This idea is part of what John McGrath so brilliantly analysed in his book *A Good Night Out: Popular Theatre: Audience, Class and Form*.

3 Motion

1   Trish Arnold, at nearly ninety years of age, taught a class on the swing at my Jerwood Workshop in 2008 with her skill and enthusiasm undimmed.

4 Deciding to be a director

1   Stuart Hood, Scottish writer and producer. Controller of the BBC Television Service; Professor of Television and Film, Royal College of Art. An intelligence officer in the Second World War, he was taken prisoner, escaped and joined the Italian partisans – an act of will, if ever there was one.

6 Reading the play

1   Willett, John. *Caspar Neher: Brecht's Designer*. London: Methuen, in association with the Arts Council of Great Britain, 1986.
2   The German terrorist group, the Red Army Faction, was known by the names of its founders Andreas Baader and Ulrike Meinhof.
3   'Fit' at the moment denotes a sense of attractiveness, beauty, e.g. 'that girl is fit'. 'Allow' is used in its opposite sense, e.g. 'Allow that' means I do not like it; it should not be allowed.
4   *Hutchinson's Chronology of World History*, published by Helicon Books.
5   'Herstory', a term that emerged in the 1960s, refers to material – diaries, letters, first-hand accounts – which chronicles the experiences of women whose lives have been traditionally regarded as irrelevant by scholars.

7 Casting the play

1 The part was played by Julie Legrand, who did the astonishing doubles of doting mother, aristocratic cocaine addict, notorious lesbian actress and the Queen of Naples.

8 Rehearsing the actors

1 I would point the young director to Lynn Truss's *Eats Shoots & Leaves* (Profile Books).
2 'Block' as a verb appears to come from the notion of shaping or preparing felt or knitted material with a wooden block: to block a hat; to block a garment. So it really only means to shape a scene.

15 A figure in the distance

1 Sir Thomas Wyatt's 'Whoso Lists To Hunt'.
2 Edward Fitzgerald's translation of *The Rubáiyát of Omar Khayyám*.
3 *A Midsummer Night's Dream*.

16 My salvation

1 Dr Gregory Pincus (1903–67) was the American biologist and researcher who co-invented the combined oral contraceptive pill.

18 The plays and poetry of a German and a Spaniard

1 My translation.
2 Berliner Ensemble, Berlin, actor, director, and dramaturg, 1952–61; Stanford University, Stanford, CA, professor of drama, 1984–.
3 Author's private correspondence with Dr Tom Kuhn, the series editor of the main English-language edition of Brecht's works.

19 Things French

1 Charles Baudelaire, 'L'Invitation au voyage': 'my child, my sister, think of the bliss.'.

INDEX

INDEX

INDEX

Tourner, Cyril, *The Revenger's Tragedy* 13, 28–9, 129–30
transformation 55–6, 112–13
Trevis, Di: childhood and family 135–7, 149–50; relationship with father 137–40; daughters of 12, 62–3, 164–5, 169, 170, 172; discovers theatre 141–2; Highfield and 'culture shock' 143–5; meets Philip Sargant Florence 142–3; becomes a director 146–7; travels in Morocco 150–6; interest in Brecht, and Lorca 150, 156–60; in France 162–6; directs and acts in *Remembrance of Things Past* 167–71
triangles 5
Twist (dance) 27

vertical space 4–5, 6, 13

visual research 51–2, 77–8; and design 114–17
vocation, directing as 33–4
voice: and communication 68; music and sound 118
voice work 119

walking the labyrinth 51–2
waltz 26
Weber, Carl 160
Webster, John, *The Duchess of Malfi* 50, 91, 109
Wight, Peter 28
Willett, John 158
willpower 33
women, and clichés 88–9
women directors 63, 126
words, meanings of 46, 47
workbooks 41, 44–52, 52
working notes 123
Wright, Nicholas 128
writers, researching 47

181

Printed in Great Britain
by Amazon